L E T T E R S T O

Heaven

Words of Comfort
for the Grieving Soul

a labor of love by
Thena Smith and Lynne Carey

For information write:
Bluegrass Publishing
PO Box 634
Mayfield, KY 42066 USA
service@theultimateword.com
www.theultimateword.com
www.bluegrasspublishing.com

ISBN: 1-59978-000-3

1st ed.
Mayfield, KY : Bluegrass Pub., 2005

Cover Design: Todd Jones, Tennessee
Proudly printed in the United States of America

Table of Contents

Table of Contents

Dedication

This book is lovingly dedicated
to my Heavenly Father,
the giver of all good and perfect gifts.
I find myself without words
adequate to express the love,
gratitude and adoration
I feel for Him.
~Thena

Dedicated to my two wonderful sons - Dustin & Scott,
my parents Joan & Earl, my good friend Ruth
and in memory of my grandmother who taught me
so much about life and crafting - Leila.
They give so much to me with their love,
time and patience. I cherish them one and all.
Also to our Lord above who gives me the words
to lend a bit of comfort to those in need.
~Lynne

he LORD is my shepherd; I shall not want. He maketh me to lie down in green pastures: he leadeth me beside the still waters. He restoreth my soul: he leadeth me in the paths of righteousness for his name's sake. Yea, though I walk through the valley of the shadow of death, I will fear no evil: for thou art with me; thy rod and thy staff they comfort me. Thou preparest a table before me in the presence of mine enemies: thou anointest my head with oil; my cup runneth over. Surely goodness and mercy shall follow me all the days of my life: and I will dwell in the house of the LORD for ever. ~Psalm 23

About the Book

A few words about the purpose of this book.

This book can be used to create cards for those who grieve or to create a scrapbook page putting your own feelings into words.

Some of the verses were written for you to make cards for your friends and loved ones, some were written to help you put into words your feelings about a loss, or as if you were the one called away and wanted to comfort your loved ones.

People handle grief and express it in many different ways. Some hold their grief inside, unable to put it into words. Others need to say their feelings out loud and share with friends. May the verses in this book touch their hearts and be a blessing. With all of us, it takes time to heal after a loss and even though we never forget the person, we can carry on with the help of loving friends and family and our loving God.

It is our prayer that those who hurt might find a bit of comfort in these verses.

For God's comfort, please, go to His Word and let His healing touch bless you and heal your hurting heart.

~Thena and Lynne

Letter to Heaven

I walked into my little girl's room
As she worked so diligently
On a paper decorated with roses
Which she proudly showed to me.
When asked what she was writing,
Her eyes with moisture seemed to fill,
And I realized that she was working
On something serious and real.
She perched there on the side of her bed,
Looked up at me as she tilted her head
And as I listened with an aching heart,
This is what she said—
"Mommy, I'm writing a letter to Heaven
Because there is so much I want to say
And sometimes I am too tired to remember it all
At bedtime when I pray.
I want to thank God for all that He does
To protect you, Daddy and me

continued ...

...continued

And I want Him to give hugs and kisses
To those that I can no longer see.
I know that my Grampy
Moved up to Heaven one day
And I miss him so much
Since he went away.
I'm sending to him in Heaven
This very special little note-
I'll show it to you, Mommy,
You can read the words I wrote...
My friend has a daddy up there.
I thought I'd send my love to him,
So that her daddy would know
That I'm a friend to Kim."
"Would you like to write a note, Mommy?"
My mind filled with family and friends—
That if there were mail to Heaven,
Love notes I'd like to send.
~Thena

Inspirational

When we are going to present verses for those grieving, and those who are missing their loved ones, we like first to share the hope that is within us. We offer you some verses of hope and inspiration. It is our prayer that you would read these and be comforted.

Angels

Angels are all around us,
I can sense them everywhere.
I feel their wingtips brush my face
As I kneel to speak to God in prayer.

I know He sends them here to help us
When we get in a jam,
And I know that there are lots of them
For I feel them all around.

I do not worship angels
For they, too, are subject to the Lord
They are just ministering spirits
Sent to those who trust His Word.

I'm asking that God send
A ministering angel on its way
To shelter you from the storm
And comfort you today.
~Thena

There is nothing I can say
To take your awful pain away,
But I can lift you up in prayer
And be with you, your grief to share.
~Thena

So Many Times

So many times in our lives
God sees a special need,
Sometimes we need a gentle push
To help us to succeed.

Sometimes there are opportunities
Just waiting 'round the bend,
That we would never venture out to find
If that push He did not send.

Sometimes what we think is bad
Eventually brings out the good.
If we handle it in the way
That God says we should.

God rewards those who love Him
And who trust Him every day,
By watching over every moment of their lives
And answering the prayers they pray.

So keep your trust in God above you
For He's the one who will always love you.
And don't let anyone ever discourage you—
For He will always see you through.

He sees the smiles you give to others
Your compassionate and generous spirit,
And every time you whisper His name
He is close enough to hear it.

He also sees the tears you shed
When you think no one will know
And through it all He holds you tight,
And whispers, "Child, I love you so!"
~Thena

If One Day

If when you awake one day
You find that I have been called away,
Do not fret or mourn for me
And do not blame eternity!
Just smile when you think of me,
And enjoy each pleasant memory
Of times long past and present fun,
For my life has just begun.
When in God's presence I shall stand
I pray He takes me by my hand,
And says "Welcome home my little one,
Thank you for a job well done!"
~Thena

Happy Once Again

Sometimes life changes so quickly
That it is hard to catch our breath,
But we keep on going in strength
That we never knew we had,
And soon we are able to smile again
And we don't stay forever sad.
Those who have left us
Would not want us to be in pain,
But to love the thrill of our lives still
And be happy once again.
~Thena

But they that wait upon the LORD shall renew their strength; they shall mount up with wings as eagles; they shall run, and not be weary; and they shall walk, and not faint. ~Isaiah 40:31

Almost Home

He had been traveling quite a bit,
And seemed so frequently away from home,
But at each stopover or destination
He would call me on the phone
And say with anticipation—
"Hey Sweetheart! I'm almost home!"
Even the puppy dogs were excited
When they saw me smiling and gay,
Knowing that when Mom is happy
Daddy must be on his way!
Oh, how I wish for every traveler
Who in this whole world might roam
That they would know the precious sweetness
Of someone joyously exclaiming
" My loved one is almost home!"

I cannot help but compare our travels here
To the journey from this earth,
Where I have my earthly family
And where I was given birth—
To the journey that takes a lifetime
To reach God's heavenly throne
And as the years pass quickly by
I feel I'm almost Home!
There is no need to call ahead,
I speak to God each day.
He knows every thought I have
And every word I say.
And I hope He looks out through heaven's portals
Wearing the biggest heavenly grin
Swings those Pearly Gates open wide
And says "Welcome, 'Thena,' Come right in!"
~Thena

I Will Not Waste

I will not waste another moment
Being sad over things I cannot help or mend,
I will not waste one second more
Being angry with a friend.

I do not know just how much time
God has allowed me on this plane,
But I will not waste one moment
Causing others pain!

I will not waste one minute
Worrying over things in the past,
I will instead try to create relationships
That through all eternity will last.

I will not waste another hour
Of the 24 in my day
Trying to figure out the complexities,
Of the games some people play.

For God has blessed us with each other
To give comfort, support, and love
And He watches over His dear children
From Heaven's portals up above.

So I pray my love will bless you
And you can see within my heart,
That I will always treasure you
And I have right from the very start.

~Thena

I will always treasure you

Going Home

If my Savior should call me home, do not be sad that I must go.
For all I do and all I am is because I love Him so.
If my Savior should call me to come to Him in Heaven above,
I will not hesitate to go—I must leave behind the ones I love.
But do not weep for me or mourn the fact that I am gone.
Just think of me as being home, where I belong!
If my Savior should call me, I will gladly go.
Do not use heroic means to keep me here below.
I'll be sad to cause you pain if my leaving should cause you such,
But I'll rejoice when I hear His voice and His garment I can touch.
Don't say "How sad that she is gone," or cry or mourn for me.
Just picture me with a smiling face, seated at Jesus' knee.
If any cross words or deeds between us should ever pass,
Be assured they were forgotten as soon as they were past.
I want no regrets or "I should have dones" to follow me when I leave.
There's no reason for "I wish I hads." I want no one to grieve.
If my Savior should call me home I will not stop or hesitate.
And if I should get there first—I'll wait for you by the Pearly Gates!
~Thena

There is worth in everyone
And God knows each one of us by name.
God knows the reason for our being
The reason why we came...
He has a plan for each of us—
A life He desires us to live
But when we fail, He is there
Ready to forgive.
~Thena

My Hope

My hope is in God,
In God do I trust.
I do what He commands
For as His child, I must.
I must, because I love Him
And He wants the best for me.
I must, because my spirit says
Faith and hope lead to victory!
My hope is built on God,
He is my solid Rock
Who will keep me safe each day.
He is my hope, my peace, my joy
Who hears me when I pray
~Thena

God is My Peace

I have peace from God above
Who comforts me
And shows me His love
In everything I see around me
For every single day
I feel His love and peace surround me.
When I feel afraid I will look to Him
And all my fears He will relieve
For the God of Heaven knows my name
And knows that I love Him and believe.
~Thena

Sweet Goodbye

There are some times
When you have had a lovely day
Being with family or a friend
That you find it difficult to say goodbye
And admit that it must end.

But what a blessing it is
To have those you love so much
That the desire of each heart
Is to stay close enough to touch.

How wonderful to say good bye
And shed a sweet sentimental tear
And know that it is only for a little while
Until again they will be near.

So should it be when death parts us
From someone whom we dearly love
For we shall be reunited with them
Some glad day in God's Heaven above.
~Thena

Our Greeting will be Sweet

When once again in Heaven we meet
Our greeting will be oh, so sweet
And we will know that it will be forever,
With parting again, no, not ever.

Therefore, I will try not to fear
The day when we shall part from here
But trust in God that someday we
Will meet again and share eternity.
~Thena

I Have This Day

I have this day to smell the roses
And feel the wind against my face,
To bask in God's warm sunlight
And to feel my family's sweet embrace.
I have this day to view the ocean
And stand upon the shore,
To ponder all the mysteries
That eternity has in store.
I do not take it lightly
And always when I pray,
I thank the Lord in Heaven
That I have this day!
And when the day is over
And the sun indeed has set,
I thank Him for the morning
That I have not seen as yet.
And if I should rise upon the morrow
And have yet another day,
Then it is just another blessing
That the Good Lord sent my way.
~Thena

God—bless this day you gave me,
And each moment that it will hold.
For it is greater than all earthly treasures
More precious than silver or gold.
Man cannot recreate it and it is fleeting as can be.
God bless this day and let me use it to honor Thee!
~Thena

From Heaven to My Child

*I had a dream that from Heaven
Your daddy sent you his love,
To say how much he adores you
And that you're the one he's thinking of.*

*There is no sadness in Heaven,
For God did not plan it that way,
So your father is not sad or angry
That he was called away.*

*He would have loved to be with you
And watch you as you grow,
But that God will watch over you
Your dad wants you to know.*

*He asks that you not be unhappy,
But think of him as being whole again,
Full of life and energy
And with a great big happy grin.*

*Your daddy is not an angel
For angels were not born to earth,
But God has angels watching you
From the day of your sweet birth.*

*Your daddy is there watching
As you live your life each day,
Loving you from heaven's shores
Which are only a breath away.*

*He asks that you take your time
And live your life full of joy,
Knowing that he loves you still,
Loves you now, and always will.*

*And when that day comes for your arrival
As you enter Heaven's gate,
You will see your daddy standing, arms wide open
In the place where loved ones wait.*
~Thena

My Prayer

If I have a bad day,
Let me make someone else's day better
And not be bitter about mine...
There's just not time...
If someone hurts me
Don't let me strike out at someone else
And cause them hurt,
But let me try to prevent this hurt
From happening again and again
To those I call friend.
Let me have the courage to stand up
For my convictions and stay strong
When others may speak against me,
Or maybe take my words wrong.
If there is controversy let me speak
Only when there is a need
For what I have to say and share.
Let my words be wise and fair
Not adding fuel to the flame
Or getting involved in a vicious game.
And let my love always shine through
In everything I say and do.
For there is worth in everyone,
Those with whom I agree and disagree
And it is my prayer that they, too
Will see that there is worth in me.
~Thena

*May the words of my mouth and the meditation
of my heart be pleasing in your sight, O LORD,
my Rock and my Redeemer.* —Psalm 19:14

A Better Place

In my Father's house are many mansions:
if it were not so, I would have told you.
-John 14:2

A Better Place

When someone departs this earth
To enter the gates of Heaven above,
We are told they're in a better place
Comforted by God's unending love.

Their life touched so many others.
Family and friends will miss their touch,
Their gentle smile, the grace they showed,
Oh, how they will be missed so much.

The unknown day of departure drew near—
The gates to Heaven opened wide.
A world of peace and tranquility awaits
And you, my friend stepped inside.

Heaven is a better place with you there,
But the loss to loved ones is so great.
With the faith and courage you always showed,
Someday they too will find that open gate.
~Lynne

You leave behind a legacy of love
As you enter His gates above.
To your memory we will cling
Until we meet before our King
~Lynne

The Journey

Your journey home began today—
You shed the body made of earthly clay.
Wrapped in God's promise and angel's wings
To His Heavenly home, you He brings.
Behold golden light and a gentle breeze,
You fall before Him on bended knees,
His home is now your own.
God has called you to your eternal home.
Pain and suffering are no more,
Left behind at Heaven's door.
Your unending faith has brought you here,
In Heaven there is no pain or fear.
Love, peace and joy abound
As you walk upon His heavenly ground.
Live in peace, walk in grace,
Heaven is your final resting place.
~Lynne

A Better Place by Far

There is a better place by far
And I know that's where you are.
I have wept and cried
Because you had to go,
But only because I miss you so.
For I know that our God above
Is an awesome God of love,
And by His wonderful amazing grace
He has prepared for us
A Heavenly place!
~Thena

Will There Be?

Will there be lakes in Heaven;
Does anybody know?
Will there be fishing there
And will there be winter snow?

Will there be trees to climb in
And will there be birds to sing?
Will there be my favorite seasons?
And will there be blooms in Spring?

I know it will be perfect
Beautiful beyond compare
I'm just trying to imagine
What things will be like there.
~Thena

The Place I'm Going

I'm going to a place He prepared for me,
A place where I'll rest for all eternity,
A place filled with beauty and love,
That place is in Heaven above.

Sweet rest and comfort are within my reach,
Dry your eyes and worry no more, I beseech.
I was so blessed to have you in my earthly life,
I knew only my God could send me such a wife.

You stood beside me through good and bad,
You comforted me when life would make me sad,
You shared the goodness and grace in your heart,
You were on my mind even when sometimes apart.

With you at my side, I could walk so tall,
You lifted me up when I'd stumble and fall.
Weep not for me in the days or nights ahead
I followed my God where he has led.
~Lynne

27

Military

And all the inhabitants of the earth are reputed as nothing: and he doeth according to his will in the army of heaven, and among the inhabitants of the earth: and none can stay his hand, or say unto him, What doest thou? ~Daniel 4:35

A Soldier's Final Call

For America's security and freedom
A call to protect and defend is sounded.
For Freedom is not without a price,
On the blood of many, America was founded.

Young men and women stepped forward
To answer our nation's call.
In battle they were the bravest
But alas, some gave their all.

To the grieving friends and families
Let them know their soldier is at rest.
They gave their life for each of us,
They were among the bravest and best.

Their bravery is not soon forgotten
As they give us strength to look ahead.
They're remembered in photos and words
For following a nation's call where it led.
~Lynne

Prayer for a Grieving Town

Father bless this town
Whose families are suffering so intensely,
Whose loved ones paid a price
And paid it so immensely.
Please restore their peace and joy
And comfort them each day,
Until they are reunited in your Heaven above,
In Jesus Name I pray.
~Thena

On This Day of Remembrance

On this very special Memorial Day
Let us remember as we gather here
Those who fought so diligently
To keep our nation safe and free from fear.

There was once a civil war within our boundaries
That could have caused us to fail,
But brave soldiers fought for our nation,
And they were able to prevail.

There have been throughout our history
Those who would seek to do our nation harm—
But brave warriors answered the call
And responded willingly to the alarm.

Brave men and women fight today
And have answered duty's call
To fight to keep our country strong,
And we've seen many dedicated soldiers fall.

God bless the valiant soldiers,
Men and women who fight —
To preserve our nations liberty—
On the side of all that's right.

Keep us ever in Your vision
With Your arms around us please,
As we seek to do what is needed
To protect our freedom and liberties.
~Thena

Thank You Brave Soldier

May God bless you dear soldier
For all you did for us each day.
We will keep you in our hearts
And for your family we will pray.

We know that you left your home and family
As you answered your country's call,
You made an awesome sacrifice,
And you are a hero to us all.

You will be missed so much today—
It will not be the same without you.
Our hearts are filled to the brim with love,
As we remember your sacrifice and think about you.

We mourn the fact that your life has ended,
As well as for each soldier who fought in ages past.
But fear not that you will be forgotten,
For in humble reverence your memory will last.

Today we thank our Father for you,
And pray that He will ease the pain.
Of all the aching hearts who so dearly love you,
Until on that distant shore, we shall meet again.
~Thena

Though you will be missed day and night
You are never far from sight
Your memory and legacy of love
Live on as you rest with God above
~Lynne

The Unknowns

Thank you to those who rest here
Whose sacrifices we don't even know
Those who fell in tropical heat
Or in the freezing snow.

Thank you to those whose lives
Meant others of us could live
Who made the ultimate sacrifice
And gave all they had to give.

Let us never forget these heroes
Whose feet this earth once trod
But whose names and heroic deeds
Are known now but to our God.
~Thena

Tears

We shed tears when our burden is heavy
And when sadness comes to our heart
We shed tears when we are afraid
And when with loved ones we must part.

We shed tears for memories past
Memories which will forever last
We hold them close and hug them tight
Seeking comfort from them in the night.
~Thena

God Bless You

God bless the mother who has lost a son
Or a daughter to an awful war.
God bless the one whose precious child
Gave their life on foreign soil.

God bless the father who watched
In dismay and disbelief
As he received the message that told him
This was to be a day of grief.

God bless the brothers and sisters,
God bless the grandparents, too,
For all of you who lost some one so dear,
I pray that God will comfort you.
~Thena

Heaven Holds So Many Heroes

Heaven holds so many heroes-
Our soldiers, who have gone before us-
Called while they were in our country's service,
On foreign soil, so many died while fighting for us.

Young heroes fought day and night
Alongside the older.
Knowing they were on the side of right
Made them grow bolder.

And all too soon these lives were lost,
For liberty is not without its cost.
And now they are inside those gates above,
Where all is joy, happiness, peace and love.
~Thena

A Town Mourns

A town mourns at the loss
of sons and daughters far away,
But remembers that for
freedom there is a price to pay.

They shed tears of grief
and endless sorrow,
wondering how they will
face the world tomorrow.

War is a price that we must pay
to live in the land of the free.
Young men and women stand
with honor and courage for all to see.

Remember them for the heroes
they were in everyday life.
Remember them for facing
daily turmoil and strife.

They gave their very lives
for people like you and me.
Honor them with patriotism,
spirit and flags for all to see.

We know that even in this
dark time of grief and pain
We will rise as one in tribute
to the young warriors that were slain.
~Lynne

I can get through the storm with God's help
~Thena

Farewell My Hero

It was so hard to watch you leave
But I knew that you must go.
I held your hand and my heart ached
Because I loved you so!
Although I hurt and ache inside
And the pain just will not end,
I sent you off with pride
And eagerly awaited the day
That you would come home again.
I thought of you every day,
And in the evenings when all was quiet
I would hold you in my heart
To dream about throughout the night.
I tried to be strong and brave my love
And I prayed daily that you would be
Soon able to leave that awful battleground
To return safely home to me.
But that was not to happen
And you made the ultimate sacrifice,
Helping to pay for our country's freedom—
Your life was part of that price.
I will never look at a flag again
Without thinking of what you did to keep it waving,
For although my heart will ache forever
I know our country is worth saving.
~Thena

With the deepest of Sympathy and love
We wish you safely to Heaven above
~Lynne

Comfort From Your Friends

I will not leave you comfortless: I will come to you.
-John 14:18

From Your Friends

We pray for an angel to watch over you
To keep you safe and warm—
An angel sent from Heaven
To keep you safe from harm.
We pray for you encouragement
When you are feeling blue—
For friends with kind and loving thoughts
To gently guide you through.
We ask for your sweet laughter
To come again to dwell—
To heal that hurt inside your heart
That you've come to know so well.
We pray that God will wrap you close
In His arms so loving and strong—
To let you feel His love for you
And know where you belong!
For you belong to He who created
The earth, the land and sea—
And He will keep his eyes on you
For all eternity
~Thena

Just a little note to say
We are thinking of you today.
You are in our hearts and in our prayers
For we serve a God who always cares!
He cares for you and knows your fears
Trust Him with your pain and tears.
~Thena

An Angel's Touch

An angel's touch is the grace of God they say,
Sent to comfort you as you pray.
Their wings fan a gentle breeze
as they guide you to your knees.

From the depth of your soul you plead,
"Just one more day is all I need!
To right a wrong, to hug a loved one tight,
One more chance to make everything right."

Peace spills from the Angel's wings,
"I'm going home" your heart gladly sings.
So gentle is the Angel's guiding hand,
Lifting you to the Promised Land.

Loved ones will miss you so much.
But they too will be comforted
by an Angel's touch.
~Lynne

When I See You Again

Do not worry or fret
For God is not finished with me yet.
But when He sends an angel to my door
I shall so happily go with him to stay forever more.
I do not worry about what the future holds for me
For I know with whom I shall spend eternity.
And will not hesitate one moment when he comes
To go with him to join the Father and the Son.
~Thena

Come Back to Me

Often times I've prayed to God on bended knee,
Bowed before him I utter this heartfelt plea…
Please send an angel to bless and protect my home
To keep my path safe and smooth wherever I'll roam.
Walking the path one day I felt an angel's touch,
A voice cried out "I miss you so much".
The voice was straight from Heaven above,
Strong and gentle, edged with God's true love.
The voice was of my Master calling out for me.
"Dear Child, you asked me to send an angel to thee.
Do you not know angels are always near to you?
They are sent by me to see you through.
When you step from my path they are there.
They come to you without a word or prayer.
They'll guide you when you stumble.
They'll lift you up when you tumble.
Come back to the path I laid for you alone,
Let them gently guide you to my throne.
I miss you when from the path you stray.
Come back to me and say 'Lord, with you I'll stay' ".
~Lynne

I've Never Seen an Angel

I've never seen an angel
But I know I've felt the touch
Of a messenger from Heaven
For God loves me very much.
God promises to guide me
And save me when I call
And sometimes He sends an angel
Lest I should stumble then and fall.
~Thena

Loss of Babies

Blessed are they that mourn: for they shall be comforted.
~Matthew 5:4

Dance Little Angel

Light as a feather you twirl round and round,
Dancing to the angel's music on heavenly ground.
Our dearest child, you have left this earth
Taken to be an angel at your birth.

In heaven you are cradled in God's arms,
Protected from all earthly harms.
Our dearest child we love you so,
Why you dance in heaven, only God will know.

Months we waited for the day when you'd appear,
Holding in our hearts thoughts, sweet and pure.
You danced like an angel into our hearts.
Never once did we imagine life apart.

God lifted you to heaven to dance with him—
Know our love for you will never dim.
Dance little angel for all heaven to see.
Someday we'll join you for eternity.
~Lynne

No Time to Hold You

We had no time to hold you
Before you left this earth,
No time to rejoice with family
Over the sweetness of your birth.
Although our arms ached to hold you
That was not meant to be,
For heaven called you home too swiftly—
Thank God, we shall have eternity.
~Thena

Heaven's Child

Some would say that you didn't exist—
That you were not really born on earth,
And that you do not count
Since you never experienced birth.

But you lived in God's heart—
And in my heart ever more,
Whether or not your tiny frame
Ever entered this earthly shore.

I have no pictures to place here—
For our little family to view,
But I place instead this little verse
To show that we remember you.
~Thena

I have no womb to lose its treasure
No pregnancy that ended that way,
But I have a father's empty heart
With a hurt that seems to stay.
I have a love for that little being
That was soon to be born from your womb.
And I have a heartache and tears that flow
When I see that empty little room.
~Thena

A Father's Miscarriage

You may not think I hurt
Or feel the loss the way I do,
Because as men, sometimes
We don't let our tears flow through.

But I marked the date on my heart
In a marker that cannot be erased,
And then suddenly
The loss of our expected child I faced.

I had pictured in my mind
How this little one would look,
How we would go for walks
And I would read him story books.

But that was not to be,
And my heart is wracked with pain—
Although some would reassure me
That I will have the chance for fatherhood again.

But as the day approaches
I feel just as passionate about this little one
As I did right from the start,
Because their name is there still
forever written on my heart.
~Thena

Let God be your source of comfort
And let Him give you peace
Knowing that His love surrounds you
And will never ever cease.
~Thena

First Birthday in Heaven

Today is a special day
As we celebrate the blessing of your birth,
The beginning of that oh, so brief time
That you spent with us on earth.
We had no way of knowing
As we welcomed you that day
That in Heaven's awesome beauty
You would celebrate your first birthday.
Are there angels gathered around you
Do they celebrate up there
With singing and rejoicing
And flying through the air?
Or is this just another day —
Because God knew you
Long before your birth—
And a birthday is just the day
That He sent you to earth.
There is so much we would ask you
So much I'd love to know about,
But that God loves you—
Of this I have no doubt.
I know that He will take care of you,
And keep you safe and warm,
And that the safest place for a baby to be
Is nestled in the Father's arms.
~Thena

Celebrate With Jesus!

To My Child

They say not to fret and cry—
That I will have another baby,
Another child to take your place,
But that child won't have your face...

That child may be beautiful and smart
And have a special place in my heart,
But it will never fill that part
That was yours alone.

They say not to mourn and cry any more
That life has so much in store,
And I should stop my fretting—
Get about the business of forgetting...

I will be strong and go on living,
I will be loving, caring and forgiving.
But never in a million years,
Even though I'll dry my tears...
Will I stop loving you!

You will always be in my heart—
Always and forever a special part.
And when I walk inside Heaven's gate
I'll look for you where loved ones wait!
~Thena

Dance upon the streets of Heaven
as you danced in your earthly life.
~Lynne

Holding Gabriel's Hands

Just a few days ago
We could not understand
That this would not be a joyful day
Of holding our new baby's hand.
All of the preparation
And joyous days of waiting
For Gabriel to join us
Were supposed to end with celebrating.
Our special little angel
Was to be our pride and joy
Our precious gift from Heaven
Our darling little boy.
But that was not to be
And too quickly he was gone
Lifted up to Heaven
To hear the angels' songs.
We know where our darling is
And we will get through this sorrow somehow
For as for our Gabriel's tiny hands-
Jesus holds them now.
~Thena

Written for Jeannette November 05
(See this poem in a beautiful layout in the gallery at www.bluegrasspublishing.com)

A tiny hand to hold,
A heart of purest gold
These memories of you
Will see us through.
~Lynne

So Glad I Had You

I'm so glad I had you
If only for a brief while.
I will never forget the smell of you
And the sweetness of your smile.
I can still feel your tiny arms
Wrapped around my neck and then
I can almost hear your giggle
And see that cute little grin.
Oh, time passes so quickly
And soon it will have been so many years
That separate the two of us
And I will have dried my tears.
But my heart always remembers
What it wished your life would be
And though we only had a moment here,
We shall have eternity.
~Thena

You Are Safe

I know you are safe, little one
But yet, I cannot seem to stop my grieving;
For though I rejoice in your destination,
I cannot seem to get over your leaving.
But God in His mercy will help me
And each day I feel Him near,
Reassuring, loving and reminding me
That to Him we are all so dear.
~Thena

God Cares

Precious mothers of babes long lost
That only your womb seems to remember still—
Know that the Father sees and cares,
And care, He always will.
Precious moms who struggled to survive
And then not have a babe born alive
But taken while still in the womb,
Babes who never snuggled in a tiny baby's room...
Moms whose heart and arms ache still
And who try so hard to understand the Father's will,
But long to know that someone cares
The Father sees your tears and hears your prayers.
When you feel that no one
On earth will understand
Lift your eyes toward Heaven
And let God take you by the hand.
Trust Him to be your comfort
And share with Him your pain,
Let Him bring peace to your spirit
And make whole your hurting heart again.
Sometimes you feel as if you are alone
To grieve only inwardly,
But know that someday you will rejoice
And have those babes for all eternity!
~Thena

The choir of angels awaits you
For they know you will sing with them in love
~Lynne

Loss of Friend (child)

I sit and look through the pages
On which your photos are a part,
And I still feel that aching emptiness
That awful hurting in my heart.

I think of all the times we're missing-
Of all the good things life had in store,
And as I sit I can still hear your laughter
Which makes me miss you all the more.

If only we had not had to let you go
And could have held your hand for yet a little while
If only for a few years longer
You could have been best friend for my child.

I see in his eyes how much he misses you
And I know that as I hurt he hurts, too,
For you were his little toddler buddy
Loving fiercely as only little ones can do!

I wish that somehow I could thank you
For all the sweet joy and fun
You brought into our household
As you laughed and played with our son.

With a gentle sigh I close the album
And resolve to enjoy each sweet memory
With a thankful heart that we knew you,
And remember just how special you
are to our family.
~Thena

To Our Baby

Is there anything sweeter than a new born baby
So fresh from the heart of God above,
To fill a home with happiness
And fill parents' hearts with love?
As parents-to-be we waited in such joyous anticipation,
Planning all the things that new parents plan
And doing all the things expectant parents do—
Happily looking forward to the day when we would be holding you..

Your grandparents walked around with beaming faces,
Filled with joy that soon they would welcome you—
And teach you such wonderful things about life's mysteries
And do all the wonderful things grandparents do.
But your time upon this earth was all too fleeting
And you came but briefly as I heard the angels sing,
And it must have been your guardian angel
That gently brushed my falling tear drops with her wing.

And as quickly as the earth below had welcomed
And held you in loving hands and heart,
God reached down with gentle hands from Heaven
And with our precious baby we had to part.
We love you our darling little one,
And we know that you are safe and dearly loved,
Enveloped in the loving arms of Jesus
In a beautiful mansion up in Heaven above.

Though we may weep and show some sorrow
And some might say "sometimes life's just not fair",
In our heart of hearts and in our inner spirit
We know that you are safest where
You are nestled sweetly in the arms of Jesus
Now and forever in the Father's care.
~Thena

My Darling's First Birthday

I cannot celebrate with cake
And candles to blow out;
I can't put you in a stroller
And proudly walk you about.

But there is a special place
Where I hold you close to me.
It is deep within my heart
And there you will forever be.

And even though you aren't here
We are thankful for your birth.
And we will continue someday in Heaven
The love we began down here on earth.

Happy birthday precious little one.
~Thena

Don't Weep For Me

Don't weep for me, mommy dear
For God has me in His arms and holds me near.
Don't shed more tears for me
For someday you will see
That I am the one who is
blessed beyond all measure—
Held close by God
As a precious treasure.
I would have loved to come to you
And be your baby to have and hold
But instead I left that earthly realm
To come to a place where streets are gold.
~Thena

God Gave Me

God gave me you
And I thank Him so
For into my life
You brought such a glow.
You filled my life with joy
Every single spot
Such wonderful love
I gave and got.
You were so delightful
In every way
Bringing sunshine and joy
To the cloudiest day.
Each day I thank
The Lord above
For sending such a bundle
Of unconditional love!
~Thena

He Cares for You

Do not be discouraged
And think God does not care,
Do not ever question
That God is with you everywhere.

You can speak to Him anytime
Whether brightest day or darkest night.
Turn your worries over to Him,
And let Him make your burden light.
~Thena

Your Life Goes On

I want to make a record of your life
Which was a life all too briefly spent.
But it seems that in God's plan
Twas for Heaven you were meant.
He knew the time that you would have here
And perhaps that is why we loved you so,
Never taking for granted
The precious time we had you here below.
Your life goes on
But on a different plane,
And I know for certain
That I shall see you again.
~Thena

When Our Children Hurt

When our children hurt
Our hearts feel as if they will break in two,
For a child never knows
Just how deeply they are loved
Until one day they are a parent, too!
~Thena

We hold you and your family in our
hearts and our prayers
For you—please know
We're always here
~Lynne

What if...

I was pondering today
The words a tiny babe might say
If they were taken from the earth
Very close to their moment of birth.

What if they could look here below
And send us a love note to let us know
That they were happy and content
And that their time was not misspent...

"Mommy and Daddy, just want you to know
I realize that you love me so
And that you didn't want me to leave,
But please don't cry and fret or grieve.

God meant no harm to you or me
But my problems He could see
And knew that in Jesus arms
Was the best place for me to be.

An angel came and brought me here
And Mommy and Daddy, she saw your tears,
And even though she did not speak
With her wing she brushed your cheek....

I live in a lovely mansion here
With such a wonderful view—
It has a rocking chair and crib,
And there's a special room for you!

I know that you won't be here
For a very long, long time
But just wanted you to know
That your room is next to mine!

-continued on next page

Words of Comfort for the Grieving Soul

-continued from previous page
I hope you enjoy your life on earth
And don't worry about me at all
For I have so many friends
And angels on whom I can call!

Sometimes we go outside
And the clouds are rolling by
And I know that you are looking up
And see them in the sky

When you look up on starry nights
And see them so bright and clear
Just know that they are not nearly as lovely
As they look from here!

I love it here and I'm so happy
That Jesus loves me so
And He loves you just as much—
Just wanted you to know!

Well, I must go back now
But remember if you will
That I loved you while in your arms
And I love you still!

Take care dear Mommy and Daddy
And love your lives for me
For I know that our time together
Was so much shorter than
You thought it would be!

Do not rush your life to get here
For I don't mind the wait
And my face will be the first you see
When you enter the Pearly Gates!
~Thena

Nestled in God's Arms

The Lord loves little ones
And keeps them safe and warm
In a special place in Heaven
Nestled in His arms.

The Lord placed the tiny babes
To grow in a mother's womb
And if He calls them home before their birth
He must have for them a special room.

I have not yet seen Heaven,
But I know our God above
Will take special care of little ones,
And surround them with His love.

So do not fret or mourn
For the tiny soul set free
But look forward to a reunion,
That will last eternally.
~Thena

God Bless the Mother

God Bless the Mother
Who has lost a child—
Heal her hurting, aching heart
And just hold her for awhile.
God give the Mother peace
Whose child you've called away—
And give her the joy in knowing
That they will reunite some day.
~Thena

Birthdays Without You

We celebrate our birthdays
Just as we did before.
But it is as if there is always something
That we are listening for.

It's the sound of babyish laughter
And a tiny giggle or a coo,
The sweetness that we used to have—
The sweet presence of you.

We miss you little sweetheart,
But we know that some glad day
We will be reunited
With the baby God called away.
~Thena

Happy Once Again

Sometimes life changes so quickly
That it is hard to catch our breath,
But we keep on going in strength
That we never knew we had,
And soon we are able to smile again
And we don't stay forever sad.
Those who have left us
Would not want us to be in pain,
But to love the thrill of our lives still,
And be happy once again.
~Thena

There is a Hole in My Heart

There is a hole in my heart
That your gentle person used to fill,
But it is now an empty spot
That only God can heal.

I didn't get to say goodbye
For so suddenly you were gone,
And it took everything I had inside
To help me to go on.

But I would not call you back from heaven
To this turmoil down below,
Even though selfishly I want you here
You are better off in God's arms I know.

I hope you are allowed to look down on us
The ones whom hold you dear,
And the loving things we say about you
I hope you are able to hear.

If not, then I will tell you someday
When in Heaven we shall meet again
And we shall stroll hand in hand together,
And know a joy that will never end.
~Thena

There is not much that we can do,
But please let God use us to comfort you.
Let our arms be the ones to wrap around you
As God's love and peace surround you
~Thena

In Honor of Friendship

There is a friend
that sticks closer than a brother.
~Proverbs 18:24

Eternal Friendship

When I am feeling lost and blue
I take a moment and think of you—
The way you carried yourself with dignity and pride,
The way you made me feel when walking by my side.

To know you is to love you
Because you are so real and true,
You are the kind of friend everyone needs—
You are there wherever life's path leads.

The loss I feel can't be explained;
Sometimes the tears can't be contained.
I miss you so much my dear friend,
Wishing our time together was without end.

I am comforted by a special thought
That friendship like ours could never be bought.
Our friendship reaches through Heaven's gates
And for us our eternal friendship waits.
~Lynne

Sometimes we need to shed our tears
Share our grief and face our fears
But with God's help, it won't be long
For He will come and restore our song.
~Thena

I Cried a River

I cried a river of tears today,
Hearing that you had passed away.
You were my dear and faithful friend,
I don't know if my heart will ever mend.

Our friendship was of the sweetest kind,
You knew what was on my heart and mind.
When I'd need someone to lean upon,
It was you I could always depend upon.

Our friendship was deep and true,
Whatever the storm it would see us through.
Like the river, our lives would ebb and flow,
But always there wherever we would go.

Our friendship deepened with everyday life.
You were there when I became a wife.
Being a wife flowed into becoming a mother,
Often our days would pass without one another.

Our friendship survived the years that passed.
Many memories of you I have amassed.
I hope you know I cherish you
For all that you were and all that you'd do.

I cried a river of tears today,
Hearing a new journey took you away.
As you sail across the River Jordan, God-speed.
Know that you were my best friend, indeed.
~Lynne

Dear Friend

*My heart is broken
And even though I promised not to cry—
I confess that I have and I will yet,
Because of a wonderful friendship
That I will never forget.*

*You filled my life with laughter
And my day with joy and fun.
We had a friendship that,
Had life been perfect,
Would have only just begun!*

*We should have had years to enjoy each other's laughter,
And bask in the light of fun that comes right after
A silly chat online and silliness that had
No reason or rhyme....*

*Yes I will cry and shed sweet tears of sorrow,
But I will shed tears of joy come tomorrow
As I remember thankfully
All of the joy that our friendship brought to me!*

*Perhaps the realization that our friendship
Could possibly come to an abrupt end
Broke down all of the barriers that
Sometimes can distance friends....*

*Perhaps God knew that you and I
Needed in this moment to be friends and that is why
Even though the time seemed short to me
He was fitting us to be forever friends
In His Eternity....
~Thena*

Today I Lost a Friend

Today I lost a wonderful friend
Who shared so much with me
I knew her inside and out
Though her face I never got to see.

I never met her face to face
And we didn't phone each other
But the bond we shared was just as wonderful
As sisters share with one another.

We laughed at silly corny jokes
And talked about our passions
For creating with our crafts
And about the latest fashions.

We talked about her will to live
Her love for family and friends
And how she didn't want any tears
If her life should suddenly end.

Some folks may find it hard to understand
How someone I've never met
Could touch my heart like she did
Couldn't understand and yet....

She touched my heart in such a way
I knew what she was going to say
It was if we were two halves that made a whole
With a friendship that filled my heart with joy
And touched my soul!
~Thena

Hand in Hand

Oh, how precious were the days you shared
Holding onto the one who cared.
Your life on earth was blessed from above,
For He gave you one another to love

The days ahead will seem so long
Filled with silence instead of your love song.
How precious are the memories between you
Those memories will help get you through.

Carry the memories in your heart day and night,
Although they are gone from earthly sight.
Your love was so precious and true
It will comfort you until you reach Heaven, too.

When for you the gates open wide
You'll once again walk side by side
Through His Promised land
You'll again walk hand in hand.
~Lynne

For You, I Pray

I am so sorry for your loss
And think of you each day
As I kneel in prayer
It is for you, I pray.
I ask God to take away the hurt
And restore you joy again
For I share the pain with you
Because you are my friend
~Thena

Time to Remember

This is a bittersweet time,
A time to remember yesterday
And all of the happiness
That came our way.
This is a time to pause and reflect
About the love we had,
The love shared as husband and wife
And watching you be a gentle dad.
This is the time to be thankful
For the time together we had
There are smiles mingled in my tears
Even though my heart is sad.
I'm thankful that I had you
And forever grateful I will be,
That though we were together briefly
We shall have eternity.
~Thena

We miss those we knew as youngsters
Back when we were brave and strong.
We miss those who died in the line of duty
Who answered promptly their country's call.
We miss those men and women of valor
And write their names here as we stand
Honoring them with a moment of silence
To thank them for their sacrifice for our land.
~Thena

Remembering Classmates

We gather together as Eagles
From the class of ninety-five,
We are fortunate and blessed
To be vibrant and alive.
There are those who should be among us
Whose lives were cut too short
But they are here with us in spirit
For they live within each heart.
Memories of fun and laughter
That echoed down these halls,
Of cheerleading tryouts
And tossing basketballs...
Of walking home together
After school was out for the day
And singing in school concerts
And being in a play...
These are the kind of memories
And others more private, that some share,
That we have of those no longer with us.
And although it is hard to bear
We celebrate together
And honor each memory
As we go on together
To be all that we are meant to be.
~Thena

Weep not, as now your loved one reaps
their heavenly reward
~Lynne

Remembering a Neighbor

I had such a wonderful neighbor
And such a treasured friend
My heart aches so inside
To see our earthly relationship end.
But though I will miss her now
On this earthly plane,
My joy returns when I remember
That I will see her again.
~Thena

On the Loss of Your Friend

God bless and comfort you
As you deal with your grief.
May He wrap His arms around you
And give you sweet relief.
Your friend would not want to cause you pain
Or have you mourn each day,
But if given the opportunity
Words of comfort they would say.
May God fill your heart with peace
And your joy restore,
For as much as you love them,
God the Father loves you even more.
~Thena

I miss you and I shall shed my tears of sorrow
But I know that in Heaven we shall meet
On some glad tomorrow!
~Thena

67

Going Home

In my Father's house are many mansions:
if it were not so, I would have told you.
I go to prepare a place for you. -John 14:2

When I've Gone

My darlings when I've gone to heaven
And you are sad that I have gone,
Lift up your eyes toward heaven
And know you are not alone.
I hope that I can look down
From those portals up above,
And see my precious family
And all those I dearly love.

I hope there is a balcony
Where mothers gather everyday,
To watch their precious children
As they work and as they play.
Perhaps there is a garden
When we can chat about each baby
That we had to leave behind—
I don't know, but maybe.

But just in case there is a place
Where we can glimpse the earth below,
Look up toward Heaven daily,
And know that I love you so!
Look up toward the bluest skies
And let me see your face,
And when you feel the gentle breeze
Consider it my embrace.
~Thena

Lift your eyes toward Heaven—you are not alone
~Thena

Lifted Up

I've been lifted up to a higher place-
God gifted me with his love and grace.
He lifted me up and set me free,
Please don't weep and grieve for me.

I thank the Lord for calling me home
To sit beside his heavenly throne.
Please know I go with a happy heart
Though for a while we'll be apart.

He had blessed me with family and friends
And a special love that never ends.
He lifted me up to a peaceful place,
So please, wipe the tears from your face.

Rejoice for me and do not cry
I am happily reaching for the sky.
Death is not an end when love is at hand,
It is just part of our Master's loving plan
~Lynne

For John

We know that John has gone on
To a much higher place,
Called there by God's love
And saved by His amazing grace.
We would not call him back
To come to us below
But we love him and we miss him
And we hope somehow he will know.
~Thena

I Walk With Him

Through gates of pearl I enter,
Called to my Heavenly home.
My faith has led me down this path
No more earthly ground I'll roam.

On earth I walked beside you
Often walking hand in hand,
Now I walk with Him
Upon His Promised Land.

Be grateful for the love we shared;
Cry not for me, my dear.
I am at peace in Heaven;
My faith has brought me here

For now I walk with Him,
But together we'll be again.
I'll be waiting here for you
When His gates open and you enter in.
~Lynne

The Lord has called our friend home
To rest in glory by his throne
~Lynne

And I will walk among you,
and will be your God,
and ye shall be my people.
-Leviticus 26:12

On Heavenly Ground

Your journey home began today
You shed the body made of earthly clay.
Wrapped in God's promise and angel's wings
To His heavenly home, you He brings.
Behold golden light and a gentle breeze,
You fall before Him on bended knees.
His home is now your own,
God has called you to His throne.
Pain and suffering are no more.
Left behind at Heaven's door.
Your unending faith has brought you here.
In Heaven there is no pain or fear.
Love, peace and joy abound,
As you walk upon His heavenly ground.
Live in peace, walk in grace,
Heaven is your final resting place
~Lynne

You Have Always Been There

You have always been there for me
During good times and in bad,
Always coming to cheer me
When I was ill or feeling sad.
You are the kind of friend
That sticks closer than a brother,
And that is why all through the years
We have been there for one another.
Now it is my time
To be here for you,
To lift you up you in these trying times
And help you to get through.
~Thena

Come Walk With Me

"Come walk with me,"
The Father said—
I trusted Him,
For He had led
Through flood and plain
And waters deep,
Had comforted me—
I am His sheep.
Come walk with me
And you will grow,
There is so much more
That you should know!
But before my glory you shall see
My child you need to walk with me.
~Thena

I Thought of You

Today as I thought of you, my friend
It was hard for me to know that I could not be there
During the tough times you are going through,
And I wished with all my heart
That there was something I could do.
It's hard to be so far away in a time like this
And I wipe tears away from my face
As my heart aches to offer you my love
And enfold you in my embrace.
Even though we are separated by a lot of miles
And physically I cannot be there for you today,
Please know that in my heart, dear friend
I am never very far away.
~Thena

Faith

Faith, like that of a mustard seed,
Is what we seek in time of need.
Where does that faith come from?
It comes from giving the life of a Son.

The greatest gift given was faith from God above,
He comforts and shelters us with his love.
When you feel the whisper of the wind,
Know a sweet Angel he did send.

Lay down your suffering and grief,
Accept and cherish this faithful belief—
To understand that when life on earth should end,
A new life in Heaven will begin.
~Lynne

There is a Light in the Window

There's a light in the window of heaven
That beckons us to our home,
That tells the weary traveler
That she is on the right road.
There's a light in my window to remind me,
That on earth is where we all start,
And it is kept burning brightly as we travel,
By the love in our dear ones' hearts.
~Thena

—◈—

The light of the Lord is upon your path
-Linda

On God's Team

God needed a special person for his team,
He knew that only the very best would do.
He searched the earth far and wide.
Never stopping until he found the best in you.

He called you home to be with him,
To make you part of his heavenly plan.
God knew your strength and courage
He'd witnessed a loving and faithful man.

The battles you fought on earth were duly noted-
You always tried your best and gave your all.
Whatever the task or challenge that was given,
You were always first to lift a hand or take the call.

With you, God has lifted the best to Heaven,
He left us with loving memories of you.
Your strength, courage, spirit and dignity,
On God's team you'll be the best in all you do.
~Lynne

We Lost A Neighbor

We lost a precious neighbor
Who brought joy to our life,
But we know she was your sweetheart
Your much beloved wife.

We lost a wonderful friend
But your children lost their mother.
We all share a grieving heart
So let us comfort one another.
~Thena

Loss of Parents

Honor thy father and thy mother:
that thy days may be long upon the land
which the LORD thy God giveth thee.
–Exodus 20:12

Tribute to a Wonderful Man

In this album are pages paying tribute, Mom,
To the man that you called Dad.
It is to honor your loving memories
Of the precious years you had.

I do not have as many photos
As you have stories to tell,
Of all the wonderful times you had,
With the Father you loved so well.

As you look upon these pages
I pray that each page will bless,
And you will remember each moment
With joy and happiness.
~Thena

Photos of Father

I searched through all the boxes
To find photos to convey
The love of us for our father
Whom God has called away.
I have photos in albums
And in boxes large and small
I would not part with one of them
For I treasure them one and all
Photos are a precious gift
And joy they impart
But the most lasting memories
Are photos taken by the heart.
~Thena

Mom and Dad

I love this photo of the two of you
Looking happy and content
And now I know that your years together
Were years so wonderfully spent.

You were not "perfect" people
Representing perfection in every single way,
But you were perfectly wonderful parents,
Showing your love for us each day.

You completed each other;
You were as two halves of a whole.
And being young and with the two of you
Was some of the happiest time I shall ever know.

Mom you were the one who instilled in us our values,
The one who taught us right from wrong.
You taught us by example with your daily life
And taught us in our convictions to stay strong.

Dad, you were the one who always had time
To sneak off for a bit of fun,
To throw caution to the wind and break a few rules,
Enjoying each day before it was done.

Mom, we were lost without you,
When to that dreaded illness you succumbed.
It was difficult to face the world without you,
And for quite awhile we all felt numb.

Looking at this special photo
Reminds me of just how much I was blessed
With such wonderful parents
It's more than words can express!
~Thena
for Kimberly's Mom

My Father's Hands

I remember the touch of your dear hand
And how safe and secure it always made me feel
Just knowing you were beside me
And that your love was enduring and real.
I remember the shape of your fingers
And how they felt interlaced with mine,
How firm they could be—yet how gentle and tender,
How compassionate and so kind.
Nothing can replace the memory
Of the moment my heart cherishes now
For these hands are no longer mine to hold...
The Father holds them now.
~Thena

You are With Me

I know that you are no longer here
On this earthly plane—
No longer can I see your face,
And no longer hear you speak my name.

You cannot hold my hand now
And comfort my distress,
Or do those wonderful fatherly things
That you did the best.

There are no more calls on the phone
To hear that awesome sound,
The booming voice that says hello
In which my comfort often times was found.

But somehow I feel your presence
A gift from God above,
For surrounding me forever
Is the memory of your love.
~Thena

Daddy, When I Think of You

Daddy, when I think of you
The tears begin to flow
I treasure every memory of you
And I hope you know.

I hope you know that I loved you
And that I love you still
That I think of you each day
And I always will.

Hard work was always in your life
And romance came as Josephine, your wife
Who shared with you for 60 years
Your love and laughter, joy and tears.

As I grew older and we got to chat
As adult to adult about life
I grew and thrived with the knowledge I gleaned
About you and my Mother, your wife.

Thank you Daddy for loving me
And caring for my needs as you did
I love you even more as the years roll on
Than I did when I was just a kid.
~Thena

You were my rock,
You were my anchor
You were the light in the dark,
I am stronger because of you.
~Lynne

In Memory of Dad

We only had our dad
For a little while,
And hard as I try
I'm not sure of his smile.

Am I remembering the touch
Of his fingers on my face,
Or am I just imagining
That I remember his embrace?

And didn't he have a laugh
That sounded a lot like you?
And the sound of his voice,
I hear that in you, too....

I wish we could have known him longer,
And I wish that he were still here
But we both see a bit of him
When we have each other near.
~Thena

World's Best Dad

I miss my dad
For he was the world's best
At teaching me wonderful things
And spreading happiness.

I know he was the very best
Of all dads in the world
And I was so very blessed
To be his little girl!
~Thena

Sharing Sweet Memories

You shared with us
Your love and life,
And of our world
You are still an important part,
For you live on in all you shared
And in a special place in my heart.
I miss you now
And will forever
But I know your desire would be
That I remember your life
And the joy you brought to me.
~Thena

Shared Sadness

Mom, I can't say this without crying
When I try to comfort you -
I know that you miss Daddy
For I love him, too.
I want to share so many things
About all he said and did,
Not just in these last few years
But from the time I was a kid.
I know you knew him longer
And I can only guess how unreal
This whole experience is to you
And the sadness you must feel.
But together we can handle this
And this sad time we will get through
For there's a lot of Dad in me
And a lot rubbed off on you!
~Thena

From God's Balcony

Do you think that from God's balcony
In heaven up above,
That mothers are allowed to view
The children that they love?

I like to think that every time
A bride walks down the aisle,
A mother who has gone ahead
Looks down at her and smiles.

I like to think she watches
As the couple says I do,
And is filled with joy and happiness
When she sees a love that's true.

If God allows this miracle
Of hope and joy and love
Then you know that your mom will be watching,
From Heaven's portals up above.

But should this not be possible
I know this to be true,
That God himself and all his angels
Are watching over you!
~Thena

Wherefore seeing we also are compassed about with so great a cloud of witnesses, let us lay aside the sin which doth so easily beset us, and let us run with patience the race that is set before us.
-Hebrews 12:1

83

My Dad

Lord, I don't know what to do—
My Dad was always there to see me through.
Through his strength and wisdom
He showed me the beauty of your kingdom.

I always knew he was there at my side,
Even when far apart we would abide.
He was a man of so many endearing traits,
A man of faith knowing he would enter your gates.

As a child he held me in his arms,
There his strength sheltered me from harms.
I would hear stories of Thee,
As I listened and sat upon his knee.

He told stories from the biblical days,
To guide me where my future lays.
He taught me to be faithful in all I do,
That courage like his would see me through.

Lord, I will miss him so much in my life,
Standing beside me when I faced turmoil and strife.
Lord, I will miss him day and night,
Wishing he could share in moments of delight.

If there is a place where he can look down from above,
Please let him know I'll carry on his legacy of love.
Lord, because of him I know just what to do,
His last lesson was "Lean on God to see you through."
~Lynne

I'll carry on his legacy of love...

For Dad

*In this book I made for you
I included those we love—
Our family who resides here with us,
And those in Heaven above.
As you look at the pages
I hope that you will see,
How much you are loved
By all of your family.*

*I know you oft remember the baby,
Who went home so long ago.
We loved her and miss her, too,
And wanted you to know.
May this book bring happiness
On your special day,
And may your birthday be blessed,
In every single way.
~Thena*

*Because of the wonderful father
That God gave to me
I got a glimpse of the kind of love
The Heavenly Father's love must be!
~Thena*

No one knows who the Father is except the Son   --Luke10:22

We Miss Her, Too

Sometimes you may think
That we don't understand
The sadness that you feel
In missing our sweet sister,
But for us it is also real.

We try so hard to be brave
And cannot find the words to say,
To tell you how our hearts ache
As we go about our day.

The years have gone quickly by,
And more difficult it has become
To let you know the love we still feel
For our precious littlest one.

She will always have a special place
In our hearts, and we will never forget
The hurt of her loss has never ended,
That's why we haven't told you yet.

We loved her and we love each other,
And although sometimes it's hard to show it
We each love you both so very much
And we want you to know it!
~Thena

God will give you comfort
When you need it most
As your heart recalls sweet memories
Of the loved ones you have lost.
~Thena

Mom, I Miss You

Mom, I'm being selfish now
Because of how much I miss you—
But I wish you were still here with us
And that I could hug and kiss you!

I know that you are in heaven now
Seated at Jesus' knee.
But sometimes I ache so awfully bad,
For you to be here with me!

It was so hard to watch you leave
And, Mom, I must admit,
There's grief and hurt inside of me
That I'm not over yet.

I cried so hard and wept so much
That I could not speak or see—
Until I felt His touch upon my head—
And heard ""YOUR MOTHER IS WITH ME!"
~Thena

I Honor You

Mom, I honor you
Your memory is so sweet
You made my life so happy
And my childhood so complete.
Even as a child I could see
That you were a precious gift
And you were a treasure to me!
~Thena

My Mother's Hands

My Mother had such lovely hands
Whose touch comforted me for years,
Wiped away fever from my brow,
And many childish tears.
My Mother had such gentle hands
Whose touch I remember every day.
I can still feel her tender touch,
Though she has gone away.
But though I cannot hold her hands
Nor feel them on my brow,
I know exactly where they are....
The Father holds them now....
~Thena

Mother

Mother, it is so difficult
To say your name and know
That no longer will I see your smile
While dwelling here below.
Your family misses you
So very, very much
For you left a sweetness
With your every touch.
~Thena

There is something so special
In the gift God gave to us
There's such grace in a mother's face
And gentleness in her touch.
~Thena

Sweet Mother

Mother is such a lovely word
And one that holds us close
To the one who bore the name,
The one who loved us most.
We knew she loved us more than life
And her life would give for each
And she would have loved throughout her life
To have had her kids within her reach.
But she sent each one off to do their thing
And never did she fuss or fret
But that she loved us unconditionally,
Not one of us would forget.
I feel sure that God welcomed her home
The same way she greeted us
When we had been away
With arms wide open and ready to embrace
And that He had sweet words to say.
~Thena

On the Loss of Your Mother

We are so sorry that you have lost
The one you so dearly loved;
The mother whose arms cradled you
And who blessed you with her love.
May loving memories fill your mind
And may your heart find peace
Knowing that she has gone to the Father
And her joy will never cease.
~Thena

Mom's Chair

On this special day
I wanted to share my happiness
With the person so very dear,
Who this day would really bless.

I know she must be looking down
From the heavenlies above us
Smiling at us one and all,
And saying that she loves us.

But to represent her presence here
I put a rose upon her empty chair
To remind us all of her love
And as our way to share.

We love you, Mom,
And ask that God above
Would bless us all today
Who witness evidence of His love.
~Thena

Mother

Mother, it is so difficult
To say your name and know
That no longer will I see your smile
While dwelling here below.
Your family misses you
So very, very much
For you left a sweetness
With your every touch.
~Thena

Daddy's Spot

Today you should have been here
To walk me down the aisle
To lift up my veil to see my face,
And flash me your trademark smile.
Today you should have said "I do"
When asked who gave the bride away,
But in honor of you, Daddy,
I walked down the aisle alone, today.
For none could take your place
And I found my comfort in remembering
The sweetness of your fatherly embrace.
And I know my Heavenly Father was with me
As I stood before Him, my vows to say,
And that He will bless our union
On this our wedding day.
~Thena

Without You

I walked down the aisle today
Thanking God that you had been in my life
Even though you were not here
To bless me with your love
As I became a wife.
Even though I could not see you
Your influence was everywhere
As I wrote the vows I would say
To choosing the gown I would wear.
Thank you Daddy for being you
And thank God for the dad He gave to me
Who taught me to live not only for the now
But for eternity.
~Thena

Mom Went to Sleep

Mom went to sleep tonight on earth for the very last time,
Leaving her earthly body with its precious smile,
And with a loving little sigh,
The spirit of my precious mom
Winged its way up to the sky.

She was my best friend, my confidant, the heart of my life,
She was a mother, grandmother, a daughter and a wife,
Who lived for her family and did amazing things,
Whose smile could light up a room and cause the saddest heart to sing.

She loved my dad and he loved her for a lifetime of years,
And her leaving this earthly plane will cause him many tears.
They were never without each other and never wanted to be apart,
They were two people, but they shared one loving heart.

Mom loved us and we each knew that she did—
We had no doubt of this
For she showed us every day
In her every action and in every way.

Mom loved to play her games with friends
And did for quite awhile,
Her place at their table will be empty
And they will miss her loving smile.

I know that her many friends and loved ones
Who have gone to heaven before her
Were standing at the place where loved ones wait
Smiling and waiting for her.

-continued on next page

Words of Comfort for the Grieving Soul

-continued from previous page
How happy they must have been to see her,
And how thrilled my dearest one
Must have been to enter into those pearly gates
And embrace the one she called her son.

I do not know if heaven has windows
And if loved ones can look down here to see
The families and dear ones left behind
Before they come to share eternity.

But I know that Mom's love is all around me
And I know that I can face each new day,
By knowing she is in Heaven,
And I will join her there some day!

Mom went to sleep on earth tonight
And left this earthly sod
Only to awake in heaven's wonder
And to finally see the face of God.
~Thena

Remembering Mom

A beautiful lady— A mother and wife,
The joy of our family, the sunshine of our life,
Left us too suddenly, and an empty spot
In each of our hearts is there yet,
For she was a treasure we can never forget
Ten years ago she left, and it is our desire today
To honor her memory in a special way.
Think of her as you read this and say a little prayer
That God would bless with joy and happiness
All of those with whom her memory we share.
~Thena

I'm Missing You, Mother

Sometimes things go wrong
And life may seem unfair
In times of stress and heartache
I need my mother there.

When life is going well
And all seems as it should
I need to feel my mother's touch
And hear her say "That's good!'"

When sad things happen
And my heart is broken in two
I need to hear my mother say
"Let me comfort you."

I miss the things that mother's say
And the things that mother's do
I guess that what I'm trying to say is
How much I'm missing you!
~Thena

Wedding Day Without Mom

This was the day I wanted to share with you-
The day I had dreamed of for my entire life
This was the day I would happily become a wife.-
The day I dreamed of as a little girl
This was the day that would be a milestone in my world.
But this was the day that I never imagined would be
Without the mother who meant the world to me.
But surely in God's plan for us
In Heavenly portals up above us
We can be glimpsed by those gone ahead
Who so dearly love us.
~Thena

Remembering Dad

A wonderful man
A father and husband
The one we all turned to
When we needed a strong hand
A great father and an upstanding man,
Left us far too soon
But he left behind a wonderful legacy
And although it has been (..........) years
Since he was called away
We who love him
Think of him every single day.
This little note is to say thank you
And bring to mind
This wonderful dad who was mine.
~Thena

God's Comfort

Let God comfort you when you are sad
And feel so all alone.
Let Him wrap His arms around you
When it's hard for you to carry on...
He cannot bring those back again
Who've gone to their reward
But He understands your sadness
And will help you carry on.
For that love you have for them
And the love they had for you
Came from God, our Father
As a wonderful gift,
As all good things do.
~Thena

Family Ties

But as for me and my house,
we will serve the Lord
-Joshua 24:15

God, Grant Your Peace

God, grant your peace
To the family left behind—
The ones who are so lonely
Missing this dear friend of mine.
God grant them courage
To get them through this storm,
And wrap your arms around them, Lord
To keep them safe and warm.
~Thena

Family

I have family that I love
Each one is dear to me
A special gift from the Father
To last for eternity.
Each family member is precious
And each has a special part-
A special spot created just for them
Deep within my heart..
I love the ones I have lost,
I loved them and love them still.
I treasured them and adored them
And I always will!
~Thena

A loving family is to be treasured
And treated as the gift God meant it to be
Not just for this day, but for all eternity.
~Thena

Thank You For My Son, Lord

There are things in my heart
That I'd like to say,
Prayers of thanksgiving
That I feel the need to pray.
So, I am putting in this verse
And writing down in ink,
The words of gratitude in my heart
And the thoughts that I think.

I had a dream of having a son,
And that dream came true—
For I gave birth to a wonderful son,
And he came as a blessing straight from you.
Your love and your guidance,
Your nurturing and grace
Put the love in his heart
And the smile on his face.

As we cared for our beloved child,
We remembered each day
That You were the reason for our blessing
And the happiness he brought our way.
I will always be grateful
Even though You have called him away,
For I would not have missed this blessing
Were I to only have had him for one day!
~Thena

There would never be enough time
To hold you in my arms, sweet child of mine.
~Thena

You Have a Big Sister

Little one so sweet and new
I have a story to tell you,
About someone you've yet to meet
A big sister so lovely and sweet.
She would have cuddled up with you
As only a big sister can do,
But alas that was not to be
And will have to wait for eternity.
But know that if it indeed is true
That those in heaven see what we do,
Then from God's Heaven up above
Your sister watches over you in love.
~Thena

I Love You Sister

I love you little sister
Even though you died so long ago,
I never got to hold you
And say "I love you so."
I never got to teach you
The things big sisters know,
I didn't get to tease you
Nor did I get to watch you grow.
But when I get to heaven,
I will run inside the gate
And look for you little sister
Wherever loved ones wait!
~Thena

Our Sweet Son is in Heaven

Dear Lord, you brought our child to Heaven today,
The loss is so deep that I wonder how'll we survive.
There are so many things we want him to know,
Things we meant to say or do when he was alive.
Please hold him tight in your loving arms,
The way we did when he was within our reach.
Please tell him we miss and love him so,
To those around him, many lessons he did teach.
He taught us about unconditional love,
To find the joy in small earthly delights.
That courage comes in very small packages,
Hugs and kisses hold you through long nights.
In the morning sun we see his bright smile,
In the stars we see his bright shining eyes.
With the wind I hear his sweet giggle.
In all these things we know his spirit lies.
Dear Lord, we know he is safe there with you,
Waiting for us in your heavenly home.
Lord, place a kiss upon his brow,
Let him know we'll see him at your throne.
~Lynne

Thank You For Love

Thank you Father for the love that this son brought to me
From the time he was an infant playing at my knee.
Thank you for loaning him to me for these few short years
And forgive me if in letting him go I feel the need to shed my tears.
I am not ungrateful, Lord and do not ever want to be
For I was blessed beyond all measure in the time he was here with me.
~Thena

Dear God,

I would never question your wisdom,
And no explanation dare demand,
But humbly God, I ask You,
Please help me understand...
My dear sister was truly heaven sent
And a treasure to us all,
And I cannot discern dear Lord
Why her name You would call.
I know that Heaven she deserved,
And that it was her eternal goal someday,
But we are lost and lonely here
Since You called her away.
My mind is baffled trying to think
And my heart is torn in two.
That's why in this dark hour
With trust and faith I turn to You.
Please reach down in Your mercy Lord,
With Your loving compassionate hand,
And touch each one of us in spirit
So that this loss we may understand.
I pray that (.........)___ is able to look down at us
From those portals up above,
To see the families, friends and co—workers
And all of those she dearly loves.
I thank you for the days we had
Though they feel far too short to me,
But most of all I thank you Lord
That we shall have all eternity.
~Thena

My Darling Niece

I look around me and the world seems empty,
It won't be bearable for me for quite a while,
For nothing seems to have that loveliness
That was brought to the world by your sweet smile.

The games the children play remind me,
(And the funny things that kids will say)
Of the happiness and joy you brought us,
And the delight of being part of your life each day.

I do not know the reason that He called you
At such a tender age to come to Him in heaven above,
But I trust that He will someday tell us,
For He is the one who filled our hearts with love.

God loans us precious children to nurture and to love,
And He knows that we hold them, oh so dear,
So I do not question His love and wisdom,
Though I wish He would have let us keep you longer here.

I do not know the rules of heaven,
And whether or not you see us here below.
But I trust that you are happy beyond all measure.
And that our eternal love for you, somehow, you know.

The only thing that makes it bearable
That you have been called away
Is knowing that we all will be reunited
When we join you in Heaven some sweet day.
~Thena

Father God, in Heaven, please comfort with your love.
Ease their pain and sorrow with blessings from above
~Linda

Please Don't Let Me Forget

If you see that my memory is failing me
And my body is surviving in a feeble state,
There are several requests that I would make.
First that you surround me with reminders of my faith,
And know that even if my ears don't seem to hear it,
I'm confident that God will direct it to my spirit.

Remind me of His love for me,
And of the love of my family too.
And know that no matter what,
My heart will always be full of love for you.

If I look as if I don't hear you,
Or if my eyes have lost that sparkle
That tells you that I understand,
Please still hug me and hold my hand.

Even if you are rushed for time
And feel that I do not even know you are there,
It is important that your actions say you care,
And that there is a bond that we still share.

Say a prayer for me that God will touch me,
For only God's touch
Is more powerful than your touch,
And He can touch me through your hand
In a way that I can understand...
if you are available.

And please, before you leave my side,
Whether we have laughed or cried,
I'm still the same inside,
And I need you to tell me that you love me...
~Thena

What If?

What if each tear we shed
were a stepping stone,
would they form a path
that leads to His throne?

What if we saw you
standing there,
would we say your dying
just wasn't fair?

What if we could take
you by the hand,
would we lead you
back to this earthly land?

What if we missed you so much
That our hearts are truly broken,
Would we seek more time with you
to share words and praise unspoken?

Or would we have the courage
to wish you only the best,
and remember that your absence
is only a fleeting test?

Indeed, I know we'd find you
standing happily at His throne,
and realize at last you are
at peace in your heavenly home.
~Lynne

My grief is for my sadness and sorrow,
but I will rejoice on some glad tomorrow.
~Thena

Not Enough Time...

There's not enough time in the world today
To make someone sad or to shove them away!

There's not enough time to speak harsh words to a friend
Or write an unkind note that you know you shouldn't send.

There's not enough time to be petty or mean,
Not to loved ones and family or to those yet unseen.

There's not enough time to waste one second or two,
Doing things that can cause heartache to me or to you..

We have no way of knowing just when
Our time on this earth will come to an end.

There's just enough time to do what we can do
To let the love in our hearts come shining through.
~Thena

God Grant Us Time

God, please grant us time
To show others our love
Before you call us to your side.
Help us to make right decisions
In the things we say and do
That will show others about us
The love we have for you.
Please let those who have gone ahead
Know that we miss them
And that we still hold them dear.
And each day we thank you
For the time we had them here.
~Thena

Prayer For Loved One

Father in heaven up above
Look down upon this child you love,
And give her the strength and courage, too
That can only come from you.
Help her to accept what is your will
And seek it with all her heart,
Knowing that from those we love
Sometimes we have to part.
But let her rejoice in knowing
That soon again she'll be
Reunited with her loved one
But for all eternity!
And until that time we ask of you
That you will hold her hand,
Lift her Lord when she is weary,
And help her Lord to stand!
We ask these things in Jesus name
And trust that you always hear,
For you have told us that you do
And that you are always near.
So Father in Your hands
I place my lovely friend,
Trusting you to help her through
In Jesus name, Amen.
~Thena

God Bless you and keep you
Safely through the night
And may He wake you gently
When comes the morning's light.
~Thena

In Memoriam

I will perpetuate your memory
through all generations;
therefore the nations will praise you
for ever and ever.
-Psalm 45:17

In Memory of Our Fallen Hero

A man of honor and bravery is no longer with us,
Gone from our lives are his friendship and his smile.
He was a wonderful friend and a great neighbor
Whom we had known for quite awhile.

Loving life and cherishing his family,
Was the way he celebrated his everyday.
He did even the most mundane of duties
In the most outstanding way.

With dedication and devotion
He carried out each task at hand,
Doing with pride and honor his duty
As on the side of right, he made his stand.

Yes, he fell in the line of duty,
And with his fall we suffered the loss
Of a loving friend, husband, son and neighbor
Who with his life paid so great a cost.

His name is now written down as hero,
But we would rather that he stood here with us now
Holding the hands of those who love him,
If only we could turn back time somehow...

But we will look up to God in heaven,
And pray that He has welcomed him inside,
And that he knows how much we love him,
And God will somehow use the scores of tears we've cried.

-continued on next page

Words of Comfort for the Grieving Soul

-continued from previous page
Father, take good care of this dear friend of ours
And comfort those he so quickly had to leave.
Please wrap Your arms around his dear wife,
And hug her close, Lord, as she grieves.

And Father from this tragedy, help us to remember
The heroes that surround us everyday
And to honor each with our love and devotion,
And cherish them before they are called away.

Thank you God that we had him with us
For we treasure each moment we had.
And although sometimes our tears may overtake us,
We will celebrate the person and for his life be glad.

Lord, I don't know if heaven has a balcony
For loved ones to look over as they wait.
But if so, please tell him that we miss him,
And to watch for us someday at heaven's gate.
~Thena

God thank you for our heroes
At home and far away
Thank you for their courage
That they show every day.
Be with them in their battles
And hear them when they call
And send you angels to bring them home
If in battle they should fall.
~Thena

A Memorial

We hold a memorial service today
For our loved one whom God called away.
We try hard not to mourn and grieve
For that she is better off, we truly believe.

Although we know she would not want sadness,
We cannot help but shed tears now and again
For the emptiness left by the loss
of mother, sister, daughter and friend.

A good neighbor in the community and loved by all who knew her,
One who loved to have a bit of exuberant laughter and fun,
She was one who always was conscientious to make sure
That first the work allotted to her was done.

Each person who knew and loved her would say
That being in her presence made their day.
And even the beloved family pet,
His sweet mistress will never, ever forget.

We think of her home filled with photos and little gifts from family
All around her as she loved for them to be,
As well as mementoes of her and (hubby's) holidays together,
Little blessings that she kept forever.

She was among these little treasures in her beloved home
Surrounded by the memories and people that she loved,
When the Father sent His angel there
To beckon her to come to His home above.

Father, God, in heaven above
I thank you that we had this one to love.
And if a message could be sent, Lord, just one,
Please give her my love, and tell her it's from her son.
~Thena

In Memory

God chose for us as sister, friend, daughter and mother
An exceptional person, like no other
He created a person with a loving heart
Who was always ready to do her part.

Her desire was to help, encourage, feed or celebrate
With friends and neighbors with whom she could relate.
She never knew a stranger-each person was a friend
In illness she pushed forward not letting her good works end.

Turning holidays into special works of art
Brought to her and to those around her
So much love and delight that
It would seem to surround her

Her face had a happy glow
That lasted for the whole season
And with good reason for she was the best
And with her in our lives, we knew we were blessed.

God called her from her home,
The place she loved most to be
And gently she slipped from beloved surrounding
Right into God's eternity.

We weep, oh yes we weep, as we realize she is gone,
But it is for we who will miss her more than words can say
But if God allows us to look down from Heaven above
We know that she is sending us her love today.
~Thena

We will miss her more than words can say!

Special Words

The words that heal our hearts
And cause us once again to smile
May be words that bring to mind
A voice we have not heard for quite a while.

Thank God that our minds can replay
Those voices from long ago
And in our hearts we hear them
And know that they loved us so!

Grandma would always hug us close
Before we left each day
And the special little verse
Was something she would say.

I love you a bushel and a peck
And a hug around the neck
And that would echo in our ear
Helping us to keep her near.

A simple little phrase
That was her parting song
And I ache to hear it once again
For it has been, oh, so long.

When I get to Heaven
I will look for a long line
Of kids standing there to get a hug
From this dear grandma of mine!
~Thena

Your Grandmother Loved you

She loved her grandkids
A bushel and a peck
A bushel and a peck
And a hug around the neck.

Let her memory comfort you
And listen for the sound
Of her sweet voice in your heart
And let sweet memories abound.

She loved and treasured you
With a heart full of so much love
That I'm sure she's giving out big hugs
In God's Heaven up above.
~Thena

When We Are Loved

When we are loved by grandparents
It is a special and wonderful gift
One that cheers us every day
And gives our souls a lift.

God made them oh, so special
And must smile at them from above
As He sees them here on earth
Handing out such special love.

To lose one is so very hard
For any of us to bear
But when we finally get to Heaven
We will rejoice to see them there!
~Thena

Whispers From Heaven

I sit here thinking of you,
Wondering what you'd want me to do.
Who am I without you by my side?
I feel like a part of me has died.

You were the one that I could always turn to.
You taught me to believe in all I do.
You'd wrap me in your arms so tight
You'd whisper "I love you" late in the night.

The days seem so long since you've been gone.
Sometimes I cry, wondering if I can go on.
A soft and gentle breeze grazes my cheek,
Gentle like your touch that made me so weak.
~Lynne

When I Think of You

When I think of you,
As I will every day,
I will not dwell upon the fact
That God called you away.
But I will think of all
The wonderful things you used to do
That made me fall
So completely in love with you!
~Thena

I love to remember the times we had
I can recall those things now without feeling sad
~Thena

When I See the Sunrise

When I watch the sunrise
I am reminded of your birth,
And the joy you brought me
In the time you had on earth.
I hope you know I loved you
Through good times and through bad,
I loved you when you were good
And just dearly when you were bad.
I know, my son, that sometimes
We saw things a bit differently,
But no matter what the situation
You were a special treasure to me.
Now I watch for the sunsets
And wonder if on Heaven's distant shore,
You might be looking down at me
And I love you all the more.
I thank God for the sunrise
And for You, His gift to me
And though your earthly time was short
We shall meet again in God's eternity!
~Thena

Wings of angels from above
Gently brush the ones I love
As they are watched
And kept safe from harm
Sheltered and from cold kept warm.
Heaven's gates will open wide
Welcoming those I love inside.
And there with God we will abide
With our loved ones side by side.
~Thena

Grandparents

One generation shall praise thy works to another,
and shall declare thy mighty acts.
~Psalm 145:4

Nana is in Heaven

I saw my mom break down and cry,
I knelt beside her and asked her why.
She said Nana's gone to heaven now,
We won't get to see her for awhile.
My Nana was so very special to me,
When I was little I could sit on her knee.
She would read me stories when I would ask
She said caring for me was never a task.

She made me little sandwiches to eat
Her cookies could never be beat.
She had all the time in the world for me,
Her kindness and love showed for all to see.
I will miss my Nana so,
I wished she hadn't had to go.
Lord, please hug her tight
And tell her I'll miss her day and night.
~Lynne

Grandmother

Today we celebrate together
All that we mean to each other,
And one special blessing is missing—
Our beloved Grandmother.
So much of what we are thankful for
We owe to her today,
And we will be eternally grateful,
For the blessings that she brought our way.
We celebrate all of the things
That to us our God has given,
Those still with us here on earth,
And those who now reside in Heaven!
~Thena

Where's Grandma?

"Mommy, where's grandma?" my children asked.
To gently answer this question I have been tasked.
"Grandma's in a very special, wonderful place,
Sitting beside God with a smile on her face.
"Can we see her, can she see us?" they inquired,
I could see my answer would need to be inspired.
"We see her in our mind and in our heart.
Our memories stay with us though we're apart.

God gives us memories to help us through
Those days and nights when we feel blue.
Grandma was so special because of all she did.
Despite her age she could be a little kid.
Remember the fun times you both shared,
And the neat things she did that showed she cared.
When you needed a hug she was the first to know.
She loved to see what ever you wanted to show.

You were the light of her life here on earth,
She called you a gift from God at your birth.
Even though your fingers were tiny at the start,
You easily wrapped them around her heart.
She can see you and still feel your love,
Even though she sits with God above.
Often times you will feel her inside your heart,
That's because your love means you're never far apart."
~Lynne

Don't look for Grandma here today.
She has a brand new home Where her joy will never cease
Surrounded by God's love
and filled with His perfect peace.
~Thena

Where's Grandpa?

"Mommy, where's grandpa?" my children asked.
To gently answer this question I have been tasked.
"Grandpa's in a very special wonderful place
Sitting beside God with a grin on his face."

"Can we see him, can he see us?" they inquired.
I could see my answer would need to be inspired.
"We see him in our mind and in our heart.
Our memories stay with us though we're apart.

Remember the fun times you both shared.
He taught you lessons that showed he cared.
He led you on adventures far and wide
And you always felt safe when by his side.

You would whisper silly secrets in his ear.
His eyes would sparkle when you were near.
No mountain was too tall or ocean to wide
For you to conquer side by side.

You were the light of his life here on earth.
Best buddies from the moment of your birth.
Even though your fingers were tiny at the start
You easily wrapped them around his heart."
~Lynne

I know that Grandpa is not here
And though my heart is sad
When I think of him in his new home
It makes my heart feel glad.
~Thena

Memorial Albums

These days would be remembered
and kept from generation to generation
and celebrated by every family
~Esther 9:28

Years from Now

When people turn the pages
Of this lovely book about you,
There is one thing I would ask—
One thing I would have them do.

I would ask that they search their memories
And remember you, the man,
The husband, father, grandfather and friend
And try to understand.

You were never just a page
Flat and one dimensional in a book,
You were life, love, and joy
In every breath you took!

Your friendship was coveted
And treasured by all those who knew
The outstanding man you were
Each day your whole life through.

This book is made in memory
Of a life you lived so well,
And even after we too are gone
Your story it will tell.
~Thena

You were never just a page
Flat and one dimensional in a book,
You were life, love, and joy
In every breath you took!
~Thena

Who Was Bob?

If you are here, then you know the man that we called Bob
And you are feeling this terrible emptiness inside
And like me, so many tears you may have cried.
But the tears are for us...for we know his suffering is over
And his eternal life has begun, bright and glorious as the sun!
The tears are for us who will miss his wonderful smile,
The joy he showed at Christmas and Thanksgiving holiday
And the time he share with each grandchild
In his very own special way!
We will miss his giving heart
Which so many of us have found
To be the biggest heart around!
We will miss the simplicity and honesty that was his trademark
And the joy he exuded over going to the games of each kid
And the funny things that with each one he did.
We will miss the fish stories about the one that got away
And the joy he found in every single day.
We will miss the look in his eyes,
The gentle spirit that was his
And so much, much more that was so unique to him.
His life seemed far too short to you and to me,
But thank God, we shall have all eternity!
~Thena

Bright and glorious
Now with the Son
A new life in eternity
Has begun
~Lynne

Remembering You

I sit and look at your photos
And photos of the two of us,
We really didn't take enough...
Neither of us really liked a fuss.
But today each one is priceless
A treasure with worth untold,
I would not part with one of them
Not for a bundle of purest gold.

For I can still gaze upon your face
And in doing so in my mind I can hear.
The wonderful and melodious sound
Of your voice which was so dear.
You were more than just a friend
You were a person so unique.
A person who listened with your heart
To every word that I would speak..

I will never forget you
And the friendship that was ours,
And with our happiest of memories
I have spent so many pensive hours.
Our time should have been much longer
Upon this earthly sod
But I am comforted in the knowledge
That you are now at home with God.
~Thena

Lord, wrap your arms around this family
And restore their joy with your calming peace

Springtime in Heaven

Our Gertrude has made her journey home
And left us here to reminisce
About all of the sweet memories of her
And speak of those things that we shall miss.
She fills such a special place in our hearts
And we loved her more than words can say,
Such precious memories rest in our hearts
And will never go away.
But as much as we love her
And difficult as this may seem,
We know that heaven must be lovely
Especially in the spring.
We know that God looks down on us
And sees our hurting hearts today
But our Gertrude is a lovely flower
In His heavenly bouquet.
We know that if Gertrude can see us now
She is smiling at us in her sweet way
And would have us to remember her with love
And not weep that she has gone away.
She would have us feel the breeze
That lingers on our face
And think of it as a gentle kiss
And remember her embrace.
The springtime she would have us enjoy
And not cling to grief and sadness,
For she had a wonderful life
And lived each day with gladness.
So join with us today in reliving
Those most precious of memories.
And rejoice with us in the life we celebrate
And we are sure Gertrude will be pleased.
~Thena
In memory of Gertrude Murial Shaw

We Celebrate You

We love you and we celebrate
The person that we knew
We celebrate the joy
Of getting to be with you!
Time seemed too short
And we would have liked much more
Before you sailed off to Heaven's shore.
But God let us start a friendship here
That was destined to be
Not only for now, but for eternity.
~Thena

So Hard to Know What to Say

Just a little card to say
That I'm thinking of you today.
It's so hard to find the right words—
I'm sure all of the trite ones you have heard.
But though sometimes I stammer and stumble
And my most sincere thoughts come out in a jumble...
Please know that your hurt is always on my mind
And a friend such as (.....) is a rare treasure to find.
Not a day goes by that he is not in my heart
And we were still close in heart and spirit
Even when we were far apart,
The memory of his friendship
is always special to me
And for that precious gift
I shall be grateful eternally!
~Thena

I Thought

I thought we would have a lifetime
To share the love we had for each other.
I knew the moment I saw you
That I would want none other.

I thought we would grow old together
And die when we were old and gray-
I could never imagine
Being without you for even a day.

But though our time together was short,
Far too short for my heart to accept it,
Our love was strong, so very strong,
That it will never let me forget it.

And even if I had known our marriage
Would be for the brief time we spent,
I would gratefully accept the gift of your love
And thank God for the gift He sent.
~Thena

I will rejoice over the times we had
And treasure the joy we shared together.
I will bask in the memory of sunny days,
And learn from the times of stormy weather.
And for each day and each moment we had,
I will smile as I remember and be eternally glad.
~Thena

Sunflower Memorial

*Like a sunflower you grew
Into a strong and wonderful woman,
Sheltering us in the shade of your love,
Nurturing us with warmth from God above.*

*Your seeds of love and kindness
Were scattered every day,
To all of those who knew you,
In so many different ways.*

*Your life was a blessing to one and all
In your roles as friend, neighbor and wife
Your blossom reached out and touched us,
And in touching us enriched our life.*

*In the soil of our hearts and minds
Your seeds will continue to be sown.
And we will remember you forever,
Because of all the love you've shown.*

*And someday when all of us
From this earth have been called away,
You will be the most beautiful sunflower
In heavens wonderful and unique bouquet!*
~Thena

*God knew that in this life, some heartache would be ours
And that is why; God gave us the gift of flowers*
~Thena

Sweet Sunset Memories

We were more than friends,
Anyone who knew us could see
That you were more than my friend
You were a sister to me.
From the time that we were children
Playing together without a care,
Until we were in high school
And we had teenage secrets to share.

You were my best and dearest friend
Who bounded happily into a room,
Chasing away with your exuberance
Any trace or hint of gloom.
In my heart's eye I still see you
Picking up seashells on the beach.
So peaceful and serene was the sight
It comforts me when I dream of you at night.

I learned so many things from you
And even though I had to physically let go,
I cannot and will not ever say good bye
Because I treasure our friendship so.
I have thought of you
Everyday through all these years,
And I wonder if you look down and see
My laughter and my tears.

I pray that in God's peaceful heaven
You hear sweet music every day.
And if God has a band up there,
I know He lets you play!
I miss you still my dearest friend
You will always be part of me
But even though we are parted now,
We shall have eternity.
~Thena

We Grieve With You

We grieve with you because you grieve,
And although it won't make
the sadness leave
I hope that it will comfort you
To know your friends are grieving, too!

We hurt with you because you hurt,
And because we love you so.
It won't make the pain go away
But we wanted you to know.

And when you dry your saddest tears
And your heart begins to mend,
We will all rejoice to see
Your happy smile again!
~Thena

Because You Miss Them

We know how sad you are today
There is no word that I can say
And nothing I can do
That can take the hurt away
And make things whole again for you.
But I can hold your hand
And lift you up in prayer,
Give you a shoulder to lean on,
And just tell you that I care.
God in heaven loves you
And sees your every tear,
And He would say to you
"Dear Child of Mine, I'm here!"
~Thena

God Grant Us Time

God, please grant us time
To show others our love
Before you call us to your side.
Help us to make right decisions
In the things we say and do
That will show others about us,
The love we have for you.
Please let those who have gone ahead
Know that we miss them
And that we still hold them dear.
And each day we thank you
For the time we had them here.
~Thena

Remembering Your Dad

Today I thought about your dad
And how much he meant to you
And wondered what I could say about him
To let his love shine through.
I know you are young now
But not too young to miss
The feeling of his arms around you in a hug
And the gentle touch of his lips in a kiss.
We have photographs to capture
The look of his dear face
But nothing can give us back
The feel of his loving embrace.
Keep those memories in your heart
And don't let them fade away
And let your heart remind you of his love
As you go about your life each day.
~Thena

The Heart Remembers

I will give you a new heart
and put a new spirit in you
~Ezekiel 36:26

My Heart Remembers...

The laughs we shared
How much you cared

Your tender loving touch
How you meant so much

The late nights on the phone
Your being there when I felt alone

Hugging you as I cried on your shoulder
When the weight of life felt like a boulder

The secret jokes and funny looks
Swapping recipes and good books

The advice you freely gave and I sometimes took
The way you knew how felt by the way I'd look

Above all my heart remembers you as my dearest friend
And knows that kind of friendship lasts long after life's end.
~Lynne

My Heart Remembers You

Although I have not seen you
In quite a while
I treasured your friendship
And remembered your smile.
I remember your excitement
At things that were new
And the fun times I had
Hanging 'round with you.
Miles have separated us
And time has not stood still
But I hope that you know somehow
That my heart remembers you still!
~Thena

Tea Time in Heaven

We used to sit together and drink a cup of tea
We talked about years past and those yet to be.
We savored that cup of tea as others would savor love
Now I drink my tea alone as you sit with the Father above.

That cup of tea and time we shared was so special to me,
It was time well spent, when life was crazy as could be.
Friendships such as ours were filled with warmth and love,
Someday I know we'll sit and sip a cup in Heaven above.

I carry the memories of our teas deep within my heart,
I'll hold onto our friendship tea, while we are apart
Then some day we'll sit together and again sip our special blend,
In Heaven, sharing eternity, with you, my best friend.
~Lynne

Legacy of Love

Your spirit remains as a legacy to those you love
Long after you've journeyed to heaven above.
The love, the laughter, the tears, the way you cared
Are all special blessings you so freely shared.

Anyone that was lucky enough to meet you knew right away
You were the kindest of souls always knowing what to say.
You were ready with a kind word, a hug, a comforting touch,
To those that came to know you, you meant so very much.

I am so glad that God blessed me with someone like you,
Someone that was always there to help see me through.
Your legacy is love, kindness, sincerity and grace—
All that shown through the warmth of your smiling face.

Enjoy the rewards of heaven above
As we carry forth your legacy of love.
Please know that you're forever in my heart,
I carry you there while we're apart.
~Lynne

Dear Friend (lost friend)

Today I did a special page for your parents,
To help them express their love for you,
But when I finished their tribute,
I knew there was something else that I must do.

I have my own loving memories of you,
And stories that I need to recall once more.
I have heartache and tears that I still must shed
Over missing all the things your life held in store.

So with aching heart I sit here recalling
The things about you that I shall miss so much,
And give thanks to God, the Father,
That so many lives you were able to touch.

I find that teardrops now are welling up
Until my pen no longer can I see,
But I had to put something down on paper,
To let my heart say how much you mean to me.

Farewell, dear friend for a few moments
Until God calls me to join Him there,
And until then I will in love remember
All the happy times we got to share.

And it is my prayer that all who knew you
Will be comforted by God above us,
As we share our memories and our sorrow
With those around who dearly love us.
~Thena

***

I give thanks to God, the Father,
For you who I still love so much!

No Goodbyes

Dry your eyes and please don't cry
Because you didn't say goodbye.
Hold onto our memories and love,
As I depart for Heaven above.

I cherish the time I spent with you,
The laughs we shared and things we'd do,
You knew my end was drawing near,
Holding your hand, I had nothing to fear.

You wanted so bad a chance to say.
Goodbye, farewell on my final day.
But I didn't want to hear words so sad,
When being with you made my heart glad.

Goodbye is such a sorrowful phrase,
So very sad to hear in these dark days.
Please don't say goodbye to me,
Someday, together in heaven we'll be,
~Lynne

God Bless the Children

God bless the ones who have lost their mother—
Bless each precious hurting child.
Heal their hurting, aching hearts
And just hold them for awhile.

God give the children peace
Whose Mothers you've called away,
And give them the joy in knowing
That they will reunite someday.
~Thena

At Heaven's Door

I lift my eyes to the Lord above
In awesome wonder of His love.
My earthly body is tired and weak
To rest in His arms, that's what I seek.
Angels gather to carry me home,
For on this earth no more I'll roam.
Weep not for me as I begin my flight
God has comforted me with His light.
Leaving you is the hardest part,
But know that I carry you in my heart.
Dry your tears and cry no more,
I'll be waiting at heaven's door.
~Lynne

My Master's Garden

I was known as a lover of flowers,
In my garden I could toil for hours.
Like an empty canvas, my yard beckoned me
To paint it with color for all to see.

Each petal and leaf was handled with love,
Just as our Lord guides us from above.
The wind would dance around my face,
As I sought peace in that special place.

Now I face life's setting sun
My journey to the Master's garden has begun.
Our Lord has made a special place for me,
In the most beautiful garden, with Him I'll be.
~Lynne

A Fisherman Goes to Heaven

By a crystal lake your spirit now rests,
A faithful fisherman that was finally called home.
By day and by night you could be found,
On the shore of the crystal lakes you'd roam.

With rod in your hand and tackle box at your knee,
You'd turn your face to the sky and utter a silent thank you,
For on the lake it mattered not that you couldn't walk—
There you'd find courage and patience to see you through

The challenges of life were many and sometimes hard to bear,
But you took the lessons from the lake and applied them to every day—
Patience, faith, a steady hand, a strong back and sense of humor
Were the tools you applied to challenges that you found along life's way.

Now you have crossed the river Jordan on your final journey—
Peace awaits you across the shore so near heaven's gates.
The rewards of heaven are yours, earned with your unwavering faith,
And there for eternity your old fishing buddies eagerly wait.
~Lynne

Written in honor of the local club for disabled fishermen
run by a courageous quad amputee.
Seeing them will touch you heart and soul.

Words of Sympathy—by Lynne

A time of peace,
A time of tears
A time to remember the love
Shared through the years

You shared a love that was so true—
One day you shall share Heaven, too

Like the sun you lit a room,
Beautiful as a rose in bloom

We hold you and your family
in our hearts and our prayers

The Lord has called (name) home,
to rest in peace by His throne

(Name) touched so many lives and will never be forgotten
Their legacy of love will carry on through you

Heaven's gate opened wide
to beckon (Name) inside

Sympathy Card Verses—by Thena

I was so sad to hear the news that you had lost someone so dear
And I know that it is so hard for you and wish that I were near.
I wish I were there to hold your hand and lift your spirit when I could
To do the things that a friend would do and I'd do if I could.
But even though I can't be with you as much as I'd like to be there.
My heart is with you at this time as is my daily, fervent prayer.

Once we were all together
And saw each other everyday
But eventually life happened
And we each went our separate ways.
But today we are reminded of a time years ago
When we were a group of friends
Close knit and bonded with each other
Feeling less than friends than sister and brother.
We cannot go back in time to recapture that feeling
But I hope that our being together
Will help you in your healing.

Let me be there for you
As you try to understand
The changes that have happened
And let me offer you my hand.
Let me be the one to stand beside you
As you look forward to a new day
And please call upon me if you need me
I won't be very far away.

Letters to Heaven

Just a little note to say
That I prayed for you today
And asked our God above
To let you feel His awesome love.
I asked that He might comfort you
And sweet consolation send
To help you through this difficult time
And the loss of your dear friend.

How I wish I knew the words to say
To help take the pain away.
How I wish it were just a dream
No matter how real your loss might seem
But even though your loss is true
Let God give you peace and comfort you.

I asked the Lord in Heaven to send
Sweet comfort to you my dear friend.
I asked Him so earnestly
To tell you how much you mean to me
And how I hurt so much inside
To hear that your loved one has died.
But I know that He hears my plea
And will keep His angels near
To keep you safe throughout the night
And wipe away each falling tear.

I know that this time has been difficult
For you and your family to get through
But be aware that prayer after prayer
Is being sent Heavenward for you.

Life is sometimes difficult
And it's hard to understand
Why we must lose someone so dear
And where was the Master's hand.
But no matter how the moment seems
We have someone with whom to share
All of our grief and sorrow
And to keep us from despair.
Let God be your comforter
And look to Him above
For He will surround you with His peace
As He welcomes home the ones you love.

Rejoice in the fact that God loves you
And loves the one who He called home
Know that He will stay beside you
For you never are alone.
Lift up your head toward Heaven
As if to see His face
God will give you strength and courage
And amazing grace.

It is such a joy when we welcome someone
And we know the day will be grand
When God sends His angels for us
And welcomes us to that Holy land.
We miss those loved ones who have gone ahead
But how happy they must be
When they step onto that Heavenly shore
And know that it is for eternity.

Letters to Heaven

Father, we come to you today
To ask that healing you send this way
For our dear friend who lost his beloved wife
The absolute joy of his life.

I saw you together so many times
And knew how much you loved each other
You were the perfect daughter
And she was the perfect mother.
Do not weep that she has gone ahead
To that celestial shore
For she has gone to join her Savior
Who loves her even more.
Just keep close to Him
And let Him comfort you
For He loves you very much
And that is what He desires to do.

Find comfort in the hymns of childhood
And let them play softly in your head
Remember all the childish prayers
That you prayed beside your bed.
Remember your Mother's sweet voice
As she tucked you in at night
Placed a kiss upon your cheek
And turned out the light.
Think of God the Father standing waiting
To welcome this special one
As she enters Heaven's portals
Now that her work on earth is done.

Words of Comfort for the Grieving Soul

Your father was such a wonderful man
And loved you so very much
Only when you reach Heaven
Will you see how many lives he touched.
We all loved him and will miss him
So we understand your hurt and pain
As you feel separation sadness
Until you can see him again.

Someday you will understand
Why God called your dear child away
But let His love surround you
Until your glad reunion day.
Don't concentrate on weeping and sorrow;
Don't let those emotions steal your joy
For one glad day, you'll fly away
And be reunited with your baby boy.

I weep with you because you weep
And my heart hurts to see you in pain.
My eyes are filled with tears like yours
And I long to see you smile again.
I pray your sorrow will turn to joy
And the weeping will come to an end
As God blesses you and all you love
And sends comfort to you by a friend.

Be comforted in the knowledge that your friends are standing by
To surround you with love and send prayers to the sky.

About the Authors

Lynne and Thena met a few years ago online via _www.pccrafter.com_ message board and through sharing their love of crafts and poetry with each other, discovered a deeper connection as well.

They both write poetry with the desire to comfort those who are hurting, especially in time of loss. The more they got to know each other, the more they believed they should join forces to share with you some words of hope and comfort.

Thanks to Linda LaTourelle and Bluegrass Publishing, they were offered this opportunity to share these words via this book.

Our hope is that you will find comfort within these pages. Our prayer is that you will share these words in moments when a tender touch is needed. May you truly be blessed!

Thena Smith was born in a small farming community in Kentucky. She attended Murray State University and the University of Missouri. She married her college sweetheart and together they raised their beloved daughter, Melissa, who is now grown and living on the east coast. Thena has two wonderful brothers, Don and Gale Cullen, two beautiful sisters-in-law, five great nieces and one handsome nephew. Her family brings much joy to her life.

Born into a Christian home, Thena became a born again Christian at the age of 7 and has never turned back. Her faith is the most important thing in her life and next is her family. She is aware every day that a loving family is a precious gift from God and she knows she has been very blessed by their love.

Thena has written poetry, songs and short stories for as long as she can remember and it was an answer to prayer to have a chance to share them through publication. Many thanks to Linda LaTourelle for making a dream come true and allowing God to use her to answer a prayer.

Lynne Carey was born and raised in Bowling Green, Kentucky, by her parents, Joan and Earl. After attending college at Western Kentucky University, she joined the United States Army and served on active duty for over 9 years. While in the Army, she had the chance to travel and live around the world and the US. She has lived in Kentucky, Texas, Colorado, Hawaii, as well as having been assigned to Guam and the Philippines.

Her favorite place, and where she hopes to retire, is the Kaneohe, an area of Oahu. She is a single mom of two boys, Dustin (12) and Scott (20). After leaving the Army, she moved back home to Bowling Green, employed as the program coordinator for the local parks department. She also worked as the computer teacher, for a few years, at McNeill Elementary.

Lynne is a life long crafter and actually started attending craft shows and flea markets with her mother and grandmother at age three. Crafting is her first love and it is what called to her after the death of her grandmother, Leila. Until the time of her death, her grandmother kept a table of craft supplies in the corner of her nursing home room. Even though her crafting days were over, she loved to look at it. After her passing, Lynne had the overwhelming urge to take a break from the classroom and begin her own business.

In 2000, Lynne launched her website, www.thecraftykitten.bizhosting.com and continues to run it today. She is known for her personalized gift products as well as other items carried in flower and gift shops across the US. In the past, she has made products for companies such as FTD and Longaberger.

Her poetry can be found on a wide array of sympathy gifts. She will tell you that the words of her poems are not hers but God's and she is just the typist because Thena was busy. Her favorite items to work on are plaques and tributes for the military. Sadly, too many have been for those that have passed on but she wants to leave their family with a tribute.

INDEX

Our Favorite Sites

- *Be sure to visit the websites of all of our contributing writers. You can find a link to more of their sites on our website at: www.BluegrassPublishing.com.*

- *National Scrapbooking Association's motto is "Expand the Passion". Their goal is to bring together anyone who wants to preserve memories. Visit their awesome site to find tons of info and links around the world. to buy all your favorite scrapbooking products. www.nsa.gs (We are proud to be one of their sponsors, too!)*

- *Our favorite place for fonts is www.letteringdelights.com. Doug and his company have the greatest selection of fun, funky and fabulous fonts for all your scrapbooking and crafting needs and wants. Be sure to tell them we said, "Hello."*

- *For the best in rubberstamps and related products, be sure to visit Posh Impressions, the website of Dee and Warren Gruenig. They are wonderful people! Please visit their website at: www.PoshImpressions.com. We love them!*

- *Our favorite Diva, Danielle Forsgren, is the charming hostess on World Talk Radio, along with the captivating Rayme Royale. They welcome guests every Wednesday 12 pm (PST) into their Diva Scrap Lounge to talk about new and exciting things in the industry. It's a fun show that is guaranteed to delight and inform crafters around the world. If you miss the show, check out the archives and you'll hear Linda and Thena, along with many other wonderful guests. http://www.worldtalkradio.com/show.asp?sid=199*

- *Scrapbook Premier is a great magazine to check out the latest and greatest in products for scrapbooking and cardmaking. www.scrapbookpremier.com*

- *Thena's blog is a cool place to chat with her. http://thena.typepad.com*

- *Simply Sentiments cardmaking magazine is a place where you can read Thena's bi-monthly column. Visit their website at www.simplysentiments.com*

- *Cottage Arts is another place where Thena's digital work can be seen. She is on their design team. Visit them at www.cottagearts.net*

- *On PC Crafter's website, Thena writes a monthly column about digital scrapbooking. Their website is www.pccrafter.com*

- *My Daughter's Wish has a message board that Thena's often shares her poetry and thoughts. Their website is www.mydaughterswish.com*

- *Thena is a regular on the Two Peas message board www.twopeasinabucket.com*

- *Leora's Scrapbook Clubhouse is a yahoo group where Thena first began sharing her poems. Check it out: http://groups.yahoo.com/group/leorasscrapbookclubhouse/*

Our Best Sellers!

The Ultimate Guide to the Perfect Word
(Our biggest seller—over 200,000 copies sold!)
Linda LaTourelle

The Ultimate Guide to the Perfect Card
(A really big seller—Just released 2nd Edition!)
Linda LaTourelle

The Ultimate Guide to Celebrating Kids I
(birth through preschool—384 pages)
Linda LaTourelle

LoveLines: Perfect Words Worth Repeating
(artistic quotes to be used time and again)
Linda LaTourelle

Where's Thena? I need a poem about...
(insightful & witty poems)
Thena Smith

Whispers: From First Glance to Lasting Romance
(passionate poetry & words of love)
Thena Smith

We have the <u>Largest</u> Collection of poems & quotes
For the scrapbookers and cardmakers ever created!

Watch for new products coming soon!

Be sure to watch us on
Shop At Home Network!
Channel # 224 (Dish) 234 (Direct TV)

QTY	DESCRIPTION	UNIT COST	COL 1	QTY	DESCRIPTION	UNIT COST	COL 2
	Ultimate Guide to the Perfect Word	19.95			Boardsmartz: Bulletin Board Tips	14.95	
	Ultimate Guide to the Perfect Card - 2nd Ed.	19.95			Taste of Paste: Poems for Classroom	14.95	
	Ultimate Guide to Celebrating Kids (Birth-Preschool)	19.95			Letters to Heaven: Words of Comfort for Grieving	14.95	
	Ultimate Kids II (K-6th Grade)	19.95			* BritWit—Photo Designs- Garden Party	3.50	
	LoveLines—Reusable Artistic Quotes	19.95			* BritWit—Photo Designs- April Showers	3.50	
	Where's Thena? I need a poem about...	19.95			* BritWit—Photo Designs- Sunset Serenade	3.50	
	Whispers—Love Poems for all ages	12.95			* BritWit—Photo Designs- Treasures Deep	3.50	
	What Can I Say?—Artistic Poems	12.95			* BritWit—Photo Designs— Seasons	3.50	
	The Whole Megillah (Scrapbooking Jewish)	14.95			* BritWit—Photo Designs are beautiful full color transparencies Designed by Julie McGuffee		

Pocketful of Poems: Rhyme Lines (4¼" x 5½" spiral bound books) Each book of original poetry covers one theme. 10 titles available (check our website for exact titles—Each book has 48 pages ready to use) *Please write desired titles in blank spaces below or on a separate piece of paper when ordering more titles.* **7.95** *Per title*

QTY	DESCRIPTION	UNIT COST	COL 1	QTY	DESCRIPTION	UNIT COST	COL 2
	1	7.95			3	7.95	
	2	7.95			4	7.95	

** Clear Quotes: Word Art with a View
Ready to use (12" x 12") transparencies
6 different themes: School; Babies—Month by Month; Military; Christmas; LoveLines; Autumn.

QTY	DESCRIPTION	UNIT COST	COL 1	QTY	DESCRIPTION	UNIT COST	COL 2
	* School	2.25			* Christmas	2.25	
	* Babies-Month by Month	2.25			* LoveLines	2.25	
	* Military	2.25			* Autumn	2.25	

COLUMN ONE (1) TOTAL	$	COLUMN TWO (2) TOTAL	$
NAME:		TOTAL COLUMNS 1 & 2	$
ADDRESS:		KY 6% Tax	
CITY/STATE/ZIP:		Shipping Cost *(Actual cost figured when shipped)*	
PHONE:		**TOTAL ORDER**	$

For ordering or customer service contact us: **Bluegrass Publishing Inc.**• PO Box 634 • Mayfield, KY 42066
(270) 251-3600 • www.bluegrasspublishing.com • E-mail: service@theultimateword.com

Thank You!

The ULTIMATE Books
Bluegrass Publishing Inc.
www.bluegrasspublishing.com

*The difference between ordinary and
Extraordinary is that little extra!*

*Words can say so much—
When you need a gift for someone you love,
share the Bluegrass Line!*